westermann

On Track

Workbook

Englisch für Gymnasien

5

von:
Annie Altamirano
Jon Hird
Patricia Wedler

herausgegeben von:
Helga Holtkamp

Lehrwerk und weitere Begleitmaterialien:

Schulbuch ISBN 978-3-14-040325-2
Medienpaket ISBN 978-3-14-062683-5
Ferienlektüre ISBN 978-3-14-040885-1
Klassenarbeitstrainer ISBN 978-3-7426-0335-7

BiBox – Digitale Unterrichtsmaterialien
Nähere Informationen unter www.bibox.schule

Vokabel-Apps sind online erhältlich.

westermann *GRUPPE*

Druck A[1] / Jahr 2022
Alle Drucke der Serie A sind inhaltlich unverändert.

Unter Mitarbeit von: Christine House, Sîan Jones

Illustrationen: Karen Donnelly
Umschlaggestaltung: Detlef Möller, Paderborn
Cover vorne: © Wim Wiskarte / Alamy Stock Photo. Sydney Opera House with Sydney Harbor Bridge
Cover hinten: © Andrew Michael / Alamy Stock Photo. Surf school on Mainbeach, Byron Bay, NSW, Australia
Druck und Bindung: Westermann Druck GmbH, Georg-Westermann-Allee 66, 38104 Braunschweig

ISBN 978-3-14-**040345**-0

How to work with the Workbook

On Track 5 Workbook has a short *Welcome* section and three regular workshops – like your students' book. Every page in your workbook belongs to a page in your students' book. There is a reference at the top of the page (→ students' book, page 12, etc.). The colours of the pages are also the same. The activities and exercises have numbers, letters and symbols as in your students' book.

The Workbook uses the same symbols as your students' book. You will also find webcodes.

How to use the webcodes

A webcode is like a small website. All the *On Track* audio material that you need for class or homework is here: www.westermann.de/webcode. You can also find transcripts of the audios and videos. You can listen online or download a folder with everything in it. Type in the code for the workshop (**WES-40345-001**) without the @ and click on the lock button to get to the page for Workshop 1. You know the webcodes from your students' book.

These are the webcodes in *On Track 5 Workbook*:
Welcome: @ WES-40345-000 Workshop 1: @ WES-40345-001 Workshop 2: @ WES-40345-002 Workshop 3: @ WES-40345-003

The **grammar appendix** explains all the grammar that you learn in *On Track 5*. The grammar appendix in your workbook and students' book are identical. You can, for example, collect the grammar pages from the workbook in a folder to look up certain grammar points and aspects.

Contents

English around the world

1 English around the world

a Read these statements and tick (✓) the ones you think are true. Correct the wrong ones.

☐ 1 In the world, about 1.5 billion people speak English.
☐ 2 English is the official language on the International Space Station.
☐ 3 10% of the UK population speak the Queen's English.
☐ 4 67 countries have English as an official language.
☐ 5 There is an academy in Oxford that decides on what is correct English.
☐ 6 There is no official language in the USA.
☐ 7 The first English dictionary was published in 1755.

____
____
____
____
____

1 **b** Now listen to the radio programme and check your answers to part **a**.

2 How do you say it?

a Look at the words in the word cloud. Which words have the same sound in them? Write the rhyming words next to the corresponding phonetic symbol.

[eɪ] ______________________
[ɜː] ______________________
[e] ______________________
[iː] ______________________
[ɪə] ______________________

2 **b** Now listen to a verse from a famous poem about English pronunciation and check your answers.

Beware of heard, a dreadful word
That looks like beard and sounds like bird.
And dead – it's said like bed, not bead.
For goodness sake, don't call it deed!
Watch out for meat and great and threat.
They rhyme with suite and straight and debt.

3 **A global language.** While a lot of people in the world speak English, many words in English are from other languages. Look at the words below. Where do they come from? Write the word in the boxes below, then check with the text.

chocolate | ketchup | egg | penguin | umbrella | karaoke | shampoo | zero

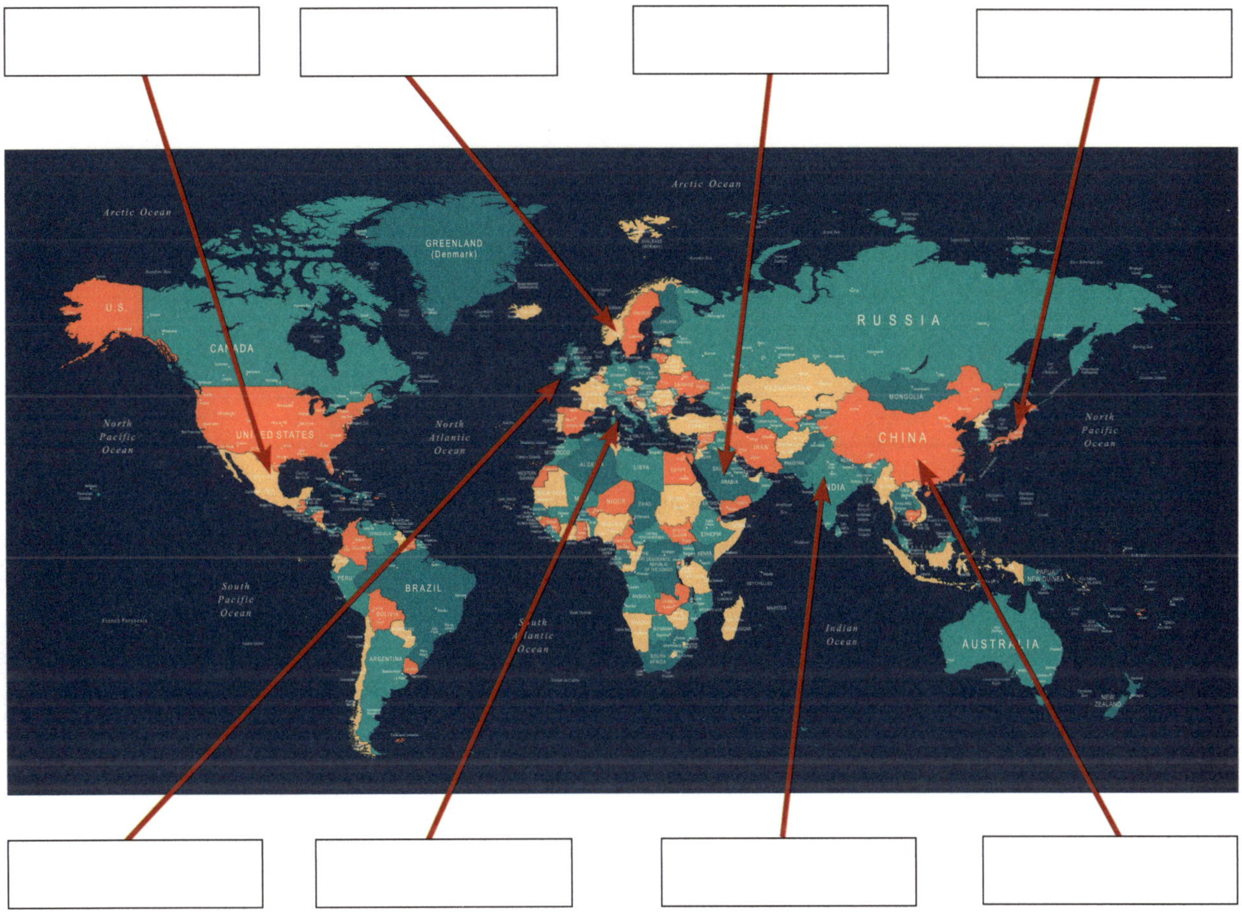

There are lots of words in English that come from other languages. These are often known as 'loan' words. For example, *chocolate* came into English via Spanish, but originally it was *xocolati* in the Nathuatl language, the language of the Aztec people, in today's Mexico. *Shampoo* is from Hindi, *umbrella* from Italian and *zero* from Arabic. The origin of some words is obvious, so it's not difficult to guess that *karaoke* comes from Japanese. But other words are far trickier. For example, would you guess that *ketchup* was originally a Chinese word? Or that *egg* is from old Norse and probably arrived on the shores of England with the Vikings. The origins of other words can be debatable. For example, *penguin* is said to come from the Welsh words *pen* and *gwyn* which means white head, but have you ever seen a penguin with a white head? However, many linguists say it referred to the great auk which was similar to a penguin but is now extinct.

Jason's choice

1 Getting to know the Land Down Under

a Listen to a radio programme about Australia. Make notes about these topics.

- population ______________________________
- first settlers ______________________________
- language ______________________________
- religion ______________________________
- sports ______________________________

b Look at the different elements of the Australian national flag and write the letter next to their names. Explain why these elements are included in the flag.

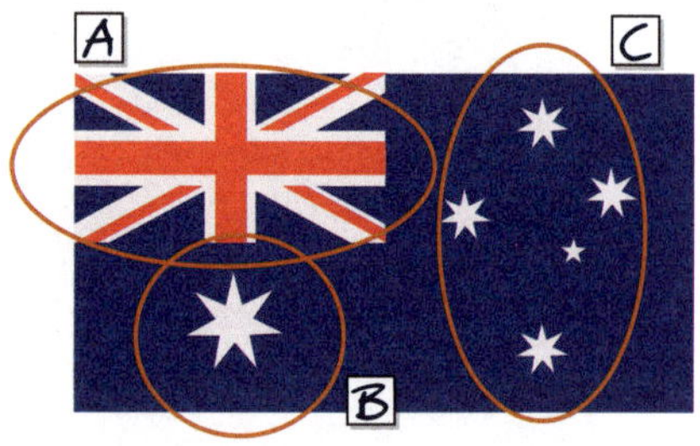

☐ 1 the Commonwealth star
☐ 2 the Union Jack
☐ 3 the Southern Cross

____

2 The trip.

The trip. Jason is at school. Complete the sentences using the correct form of the present perfect or present perfect progressive.

1 Jason ______________ (*think*) about the trip to New Zealand all morning.
2 He ______________ (*not pay*) much attention to Mrs Gallagher and she ______________ (*tell*) him twice to concentrate.
3 He ______________ (*look forward to*) going to Sydney with Nick and Eleni for so long. They ______________ (*already plan*) what to do there.
4 Jason and Eleni ______________ (*talk*) for a few minutes, but Jason ______________ (*not mention*) the trip to New Zealand because he ______________ (*not make*) a decision yet.
5 Jason and Ricky ______________ (*play*) rugby together for years, but this is the first time they ______________ (*have*) the chance to play against a team from another country.

3 **Sydney or New Zealand?** Complete the text with the verbs from the box in the correct form: simple past, past progressive, present perfect or present perfect progressive.

announce ■ not be ■ cheer ■ have ■ invite ■ look forward to ■ make ■ notice ■ plan ■ talk ■ tell ■ win

After training, Coach Hansen ______________ (1) an announcement: a school in New Zealand had invited them to play in their rugby tournament. Everyone ______________ (2) really loudly. They ______________ (3) about how they would beat the Kiwis when the coach ______________ (4) the dates. 'Great,' said Ricky. 'I ______________ (5) to New Zealand before.' 'Me neither,' thought Jason. 'But that's the same date as my Sydney trip. I ______________ (6) going there for weeks.' While the Turners ______________ (7) dinner, Jason ______________ (8) them the news. His dad was so happy. 'Your team ______________ (9) every game so far this season. I'm sure you'll win in New Zealand, too.' Then he ______________ (10) that Jason didn't look very happy. 'What's up, Jason?' he asked. 'Nick and Eleni ______________ (11) me to their birthday party in Sydney,' explained Jason. 'It's at the same time. We ______________ (12) it for weeks.'

4 **What the future holds.** Complete Jason's and Eleni's conversation about their trips with *half a / an*, *quite a / an* and *such a / an*.

Eleni I have ______________ (1) hour before my next class. Let's go to the cafeteria.

Jason Sure. I wanted to ask you about your trip to Greece anyway.

Eleni Well, as you can guess, it was ______________ (2) shock to find out that my aunt is ill, but it's great that we can all go and see her.

Jason I know. Of course, it's ______________ (3) shame that we can't celebrate your birthdays together on the day, but we can meet up when we all get back.

Eleni Yes, but the New Zealand trip is ______________ (4) fantastic opportunity. So, when do you start practising?

Jason Tomorrow. We have ______________ (5) hard training programme. And I plan to eat more healthily.

Eleni That will be ______________ (6) challenge for you!

Jason No worries. So, how about ______________ (7) pizza each?

Eleni That's not ______________ (8) good idea if you want to get fit!

Practice: Impressions of Australia

5 **The story of Australian English.** Read part of an *Australian News* interview. Complete it with the present perfect or present perfect progressive form of the verbs in brackets.

News — Why do we Australians speak the way we do? Over the last few days, we ________________ (1) (*ask*) people this question and we ________________ (2) (*receive*) different answers. Therefore, we ________________ (3) (*invite*) Professor Wilson today to explain the development and current use of Australian English. Professor Wilson ________________ (4) (*study*) the way we speak for many years and he ________________ (5) (*write*) a book, *The Story of Australian English*, which ________________ (6) (*just be published*). So, Professor Wilson, how did we start speaking English the way we do?

Prof. W. — English arrived here in Australia approximately 200 years ago and, since that time, it ________________ (7) (*develop*) into the language we speak today. When European settlers arrived in 1788 from different dialect areas across England, they brought their particular ways of speaking English. Since then, we ________________ (8) (*use*) a mixture of words and phrases that together make a 'common' language. English dialect words, military terms and indigenous language ________________ (9) (*also be added*) to Australian vocabulary, making it the rich language it is today.

News — In your opinion, will Australian English continue to change?

Prof. W. — Yes, all languages change and develop. That's what keeps them 'alive'. Australian English ________________ (10) (*change*) for the last couple of centuries and, of course, in addition it ________________ (11) (*recently incorporate*) new words from the languages spoken by immigrants. So yes, I'm sure it will go on developing and changing in the future.

6 **School of the Air.** The School of the Air is the only way in which many children have access to education. Read the text and write the letters A – H for the phrases in the correct place.

A Australia still has to overcome
B broadcast lessons to children
C evidence shows a link between
D has made it possible
E which reduces isolation
F an interactive white board with a chat
G the head of the South Australia Flying Doctor Service
H with those in rural and remote areas

The School of the Air was started in 1950 by Adelaide Miethke, _____ (1). She used the radio network to _____ (2). The first broadcasts took place in Alice Springs in 1951. There are now about 25 distance schools. In 2002, the School of the Air went online using a programme called CENTA which works like _____ (3). Other programmes like Moodle or Skype are also used. Nowadays, the network _____ (4) for children to communicate with teachers and with each other every day, _____ (5). However, _____ (6) the challenge of providing quality education to students outside urban centres. _____ (7) where Australians live and their outcomes at all stages of education, _____ (8) doing worse than students in urban areas.

7 **Noah's school day.** Noah is a School of the Air student. Read about his typical school day and complete it with the correct form of the phrasal verbs in the box. There are two you do not need.

clean up ■ find out ■ gather around ■ go ahead ■ look forward to ■ pay for ■ put off ■ rush off ■ sit down ■ turn on

Noah lives in the bush with his family. His parents can't ____________________ (1) a boarding school, so he has lessons via the School of the Air. From Monday to Friday, Noah gets up early, has breakfast, then he helps to ____________________ (2) before going to his bedroom. He ____________________ (3) the computer and ____________________ (4) for his first lesson. He ______________________________ (5) Wednesdays when he has his favourite classes: science and history. He loves ________________________ (6) about the Australian past and he never ____________________ (7) doing his science projects like he does with maths! At midday, all the family ______________________________ (8) the table to enjoy lunch together.

8 WRITING FOCUS: Torres Strait Islands

a You have been asked to write an article for an international website. One of your classmates has given you some tips. Complete them with the words and phrases from the box.

anecdotes ■ audience ■ comparisons ■ directly ■ emotional ■ indirect questions ■ 'you' or 'we' ■ informal ■ positive or negative words ■ pronouns

1 Think of your ______________________, remember it's an article for young people, and use an ______________________ style.

2 Speak ______________________ to your readers. Use ______________________ like 'I' ______________________.

3 Use ______________________ to keep readers interested and get them thinking.

4 Make sure to include some stories or ______________________ to have an ______________________ effect.

5 Include both ______________________ to show that you are honest and balanced.

6 Use ______________________ to help readers understand your message.

b You have decided to write about the Torres Strait Islands in Australia. Go online and do some research. Make notes using the ideas below and remember the tips to make your article interesting. Then write your article (150 words).

- Location / Why is it part of Australia?
- The flag: symbolism?
- Are Torres Strait Islanders Aboriginal?
- Why you should go there?

____

____

____

____

____

____

____

____

____

A new life Down Under

9 **Who's who?** Watch the video, then outline the importance of these people in your exercise book.

1 Willem Janzoon
2 Abel Tasman
3 William Dampier
4 James Cook
5 Lord Sydney
6 Arthur Philip
7 George Vancouver
8 Edmund Lockyer
9 Sir Edmund Barton

10 **Undiscovered land.** Read the summary about the history of Australia and complete it with the past perfect or past perfect progressive form of the verbs in brackets.

By the time all the continents ____________________ (1) (*be explored*), Australia was still undiscovered. Before the first Europeans arrived, the first humans ____________________ (2) (*live*) in Australia for thousands of years. The earliest migrants ____________________ (3) (*travel*) from Central Africa and across Asia before they arrived in Australia. By the time the British arrived, the Aboriginal tribes ____________________ (4) (*organize*) themselves into regional groups and the population ____________________ (5) (*reach*) over a million. Before Dutch explorers arrived at the coast of Australia in 1606, the Portuguese ____________________ (6) (*create*) a series of maps that documented the territories they ____________________ (7) (*explore*) for many years. A 16th century map showed a mysterious land that the Portuguese ____________________ (8) (*find*) which they ____________________ (9) (*call*) Java La Grande. The Portuguese were very experienced and highly skilled sailors. They ____________________ (10) (*sail*) along the Atlantic coasts of Africa, the Indian Ocean and western Asia for almost a century before Columbus discovered America in 1492. By the time the English sent an expedition to Australia in the early 18th century, the Dutch ____________________ (11) (*explore*) parts of the country and ____________________ (12) (*discover*) Tasmania. By the end of the century, Captain Cook ____________________ (13) (*disembark*) in present-day New South Wales and ____________________ (14) (*found*) Sydney.

11 Migrating to Australia

4 **a** Keira and Fred are asking Jason about his grandparents. Listen to the first part of the conversation and do the tasks.

1 Explain why Jason's grandparents decided to migrate to Australia.

____

____

______________________________.

2 Describe how the Assisted Passage Scheme worked.

____

______________________________.

5 **b** Listen to the second part of the conversation and do the tasks using the information you hear.

1 Describe why Jason's grandma said her heart sank when the ship was about to sail away.

____

______________________________.

2 Say why Fred tells Keira not to be silly.

____

______________________________.

3 Summarize why so many people decided to move to Australia.

____

______________________________.

4 Outline what the 'whinging Poms' are.

____

______________________________.

5 Explain what the expression means nowadays.

____

______________________________.

6 Outline what the 'Jennings Germans' are.

____

______________________________.

Practice: First Nations

12 **SPEAKING FOCUS: Australian Aboriginal mythology**

a Before you listen to a podcast about Australian Aboriginal mythology, look at these paintings and discuss with a partner what you think they represent.

6 **b** Listen and check your ideas.

6 **c** Listen again and do the following tasks.

1 Summarize what the 'Dreamtime' is.

____

____.

2 Explain who Baiame is.

____

____.

3 Outline what the Rainbow Serpent is.

____

____.

4 Describe the meaning of rainbows for Aboriginal people.

____

____.

d Do some research about other Aborigine myths. Then make notes and use them to prepare a text for a short podcast (120 words). Record your podcast and share it. Here are some ideas:

- how the kangaroo got her pouch
- the Emu in the Sky
- Tiddalick the Frog
- the Yowie

13 **Aboriginal Australians.** Complete the sentences about Aboriginal Australians with the past perfect or past perfect progressive form of the verbs in brackets.

1 Aboriginal Australians are split into two groups: Aboriginals related to those who _______________ (*already live*) in Australia for ages when Britain began colonizing the island in 1788, and Torres Strait Islanders who descended from residents of the Torres Strait Islands, part of modern-day Queensland.

2 The earliest migrants _______________ (*live*) in Africa for about 70,000 years before they moved to Australia.

3 The Aboriginal population _______________ (*reach*) about one million by the time the British began colonizing Australia. However, by 1900, the population _______________ (*fall*) by 90%.

4 By 1970, the government _______________ (*remove*) between 10% and 33% of Aboriginal Australian children from their homes and _______________ (*put*) them in adoptive families or institutions.

5 Most Aboriginal Australians _______________ (*not have*) any voting rights or full citizenship before a law was passed in 1967.

14 **Aboriginal Australians today**

a Add prefixes and suffixes to make negative nouns and adjectives.

NOUN	NEGATIVE NOUN	NEGATIVE ADJECTIVE
advantage		----
equal		
employ		

b Complete this table to make verbs, nouns and adjectives.

VERB	NOUN	ADJECTIVE
----	Aborigine	
assist		----
inquire		----
expect		----
govern		----
improve		----
----		literate
----	nation	
populate		----
suspect		

c Use the correct form of the words in **a** and **b** to complete the text opposite.

Closing The Gap: Australia's indigenous inequality 'not good enough'

Although Australia has made progress in improving education for indigenous people, it is still ____________________ (1) (*equal*) in many areas, [...]. According to the Closing The Gap report, life ________________ (2) (*expect*) and ____________________ (3) (*literate*) rates remain lower for indigenous Australians while ____________________________ (4) (*employ*) rates soar. Australia's Prime Minister [...] told parliament on Tuesday: 'The results are not good enough.' He called the ________________________ (5) (*advantage*) suffered by indigenous children a '____________________ (6) (*nation*) shame'. The previous 'top-down, ________________________ (7) (*govern*) knows best approach' had failed, he said. [...]

In the past three decades, more than 400 ____________________ (8) (*Aborigine*) people have died in custody [...], despite findings [...] from an ________________ ________________ (9) (*inquire*) in 1991. Many [...] died under ____________ ______________ (10) (*suspect*) circumstances, and some due to a lack of medical ________________________ (11) (*assist*). [...]

The report tracks targets set in 2008 aimed at reducing ________________ (12) (*equal*). [...] Aboriginal Australians and Torres Strait Islanders, who together make up 3% of Australia's ___________________________ (13) (*populate*), continue to experience high levels of ________________________ (14) (*advantage*). [...]

According to Prime Minister Scott Morrison, progress had been made over the last twelve years in some areas. For example, 20% more indigenous people now finish high school. However, more [...] autonomy is needed to see any ______________ (15) (*improve*) in other areas, he said. [...]

Adapted from: www.bbc.com

Understand new words and phrases

15 **Australian history.** Read the article and match the headings to the paragraphs.

Gold discoveries ■ How it all started ■ Immigration ■ Impact ■ Life on the fields

Australian gold rushes

1 ______________________: One of the biggest gold rushes in history started in 1851 in New South Wales, Australia. A **prospector** discovered gold in a waterhole near Bathurst. This transformed the colonies. Thousands of 'diggers' came to Australia to work long hours in overcrowded and dangerous conditions in the hope of becoming rich.

2 ______________________: Gold had already been found. In 1823, a convict who found gold received 150 **lashes** with a whip because the authorities believed he had stolen it. In 1839, Count Paul Strzelecki, a Polish aristocrat and explorer, found gold in the Australian Alps. However, the government kept it a secret because they were afraid that a gold discovery would result in increased crime.

3 ______________________: The discoveries attracted people from around the world. In 20 years, immigration quadrupled Australia's population, which also began to diversify. The majority of new immigrants came from the UK, along with others from the United States, Germany, France, Italy, Poland, Hungary and China.

4 ______________________: Living conditions on the goldfields were **harsh**. Prospectors travelled long distances on foot, carrying their possessions as horse transportation was expensive. Once they arrived, they had to set up tents for shelter, which provided little protection from snakes and insects. Food was scarce and expensive. Water was polluted by the mining process and had to be boiled to make it safe to drink. Infectious diseases spread easily.

5 ______________________: The gold rushes had a profound social, political and economic effect on Australia. The mainly British society of the colonies became more diverse and some immigrants became **prominent** in business, law or politics. The gold rushes **spurred** the exploration and settlement of remote lands and the economic boost caused by gold discoveries was crucial in the modernization of colonial Australia.

16 **The meaning of words**

a Make a list of the words you don't know, then use the tips to work out the meaning. Are the words in **bold** on your list? Match them to the correct definitions.

- Look for a similar word in German or another language.
- Try to guess the meaning of the words before or after it.
- Do you already know part of the word or another form of the word?

1 unpleasant and difficult to live in: ______________________
2 a person who searches an area for minerals, oil, etc.: ______________________
3 cause something to happen: ______________________
4 a hit with a whip or thin stick: ______________________
5 important and well known: ______________________

b Find these words in the text and write a definition in your own words. Use your exercise book.

- waterhole
- whip
- scarce
- boost

Discovering Australia

17 **A symbol of Australia.** Read this article about one of the symbols of Australia: the boomerang. Complete it with the correct passive form of the verbs in brackets.

Boomerangs ______________________ (1) (*consider*) to be the earliest flying machines invented by humans and ____________________________ (2) (*usually associate*) with Australian Aborigines. In fact, Australian Aboriginal boomerangs that are ten thousand years old __________________________________ (3) (*find*). The name 'boomerang' comes from the language of the indigenous Australian Turuwal tribe of Aborigines who lived south of Sydney. However, the boomerang did not originate in Australia. Older hunting boomerangs ____________________________ (4) (*discover*) throughout Europe. One boomerang that __________________________ (5) (*find*) in a cave in Poland ____________________________ (6) (*make*) of mammoth's tusk and it ____________________________ (7) (*believe*) to be about 30,000 years old. No one knows for sure how the returning boomerang ______________________ (8) (*invent*). It __________________________ (9) (*possibly discover*) by accident by an early hunter trying to improve a hunting stick that ___________________________ (10) (*still use*) today by the Australian Aborigines and by the Navajo Indians in America. The modern boomerang _______________________ (11) (*associate*) with Australia because it ___________________________________ (12) (*preserve*) by Australian Aborigines who never used a bow and arrow for hunting.

18 **Myths and mythical creatures**

a Australia is a land of myths and legends. Choose the correct forms to complete this text.

The Hawkesbury River Monster is the Australian version of the Loch Ness Monster. This creature **says / is said** (1) to live in the waters of the Hawkesbury River in New South Wales. It **has been described / have been described** (2) as a grey or black snake-like creature about nine metres long. Paintings of the monster dating back thousands of years **have discovered / have been discovered** (3) in caves. The drop bear is one of Australia's creepiest urban legends. This creature is a terrifying version of the koala. These bears **is believed / are believed** (4) to have dark hair, powerful arms and large teeth. People **say / are said** (5) that drop bears, which are as big as leopards, live in treetops and drop down on their victims. The bunyip is a spirit monster which **is known / are known** (6) to sleep in rivers in the day and come out at night looking for people and animals **to eat / to be eaten** (7). It **is thought / are thought** (8) to have a face like a dog, dark fur, flippers, tusks and a horse-like tail.

»» **b** Are there similar mythical creatures in Germany? Do some research and write a blogpost (150 words) in your exercise book. Include at least five passive forms.

19 **Australian Aboriginal sacred sites and tourism.** Read the text about sacred places in Australia. Complete it with the words in brackets and the active or passive form of the verbs in the box.

affect ■ ban ■ cause ■ close ■ contribute ■ discover ■ know ■ list ■ locate ■ need ■ preserve ■ register ■ respect ■ see ■ try ■ visit

The two most famous Aboriginal sacred places in Australia are perhaps Uluru and the Great Barrier Reef, but there are many others. Sometimes, they ____________________ (1) by accident or they are identified by the elders of the tribes.

Baiame Cave ____________________ (2) in Singleton Council in New South Wales, overlooking a valley. An exceptionally rare and unique art representation of Baiame, the 'Creator', can ____________________ (3) on a rock wall at the back of the cave.

There are several elements around the figure's body including boomerangs, an axe and possibly a spear. The cave ____________________ (*highly*) (4) by the local Wonnarua people, numerous Aboriginal nations throughout south-east Australia and the wider community of the Hunter Valley. It ____________________ (*also*) (5) by many tourists as it ____________________ (6) on many tourist information websites.

Unfortunately, the paintings have become damaged over the years.

The cave, which ____________________ (7) as an Aboriginal Place, is listed as a State significant heritage item and ____________________ (8) urgent protection.

Aboriginal groups across Australia are concerned about protecting sacred sites and ____________________ (9) to limit public access to ensure these areas of historical and spiritual importance ____________________ (10) and not invaded by tourists.

In 2019, tourists ____________________ (11) from climbing Uluru. More recently, more than one third of the Grampians National Park, another area full of Aboriginal heritage which ____________________ (12) as an international climbing destination, ____________________ (13) for climbing.

Although tourism can be a good source of income for a country, the excess of tourism or 'overtourism' can have a negative impact. In terms of environmental impact, overtourism ____________________ (14) to an increase in water consumption, air pollution and waste in tourist destinations as well as potential destruction of natural and historical sites. It ____________________ (15) difficulties for the local population as their quality of life ____________________ (16), often due to an increase in prices, e.g. of food and housing.

Practice: Climate reality

a platypus

20 The impacts of climate change

a Skim the article and find a suitable headline.

____

The most obvious impacts of climate change in Australia ______________ (1) (*see*) in the natural environment and ______________ (2) (*associate*) with increasingly warm temperatures and more severe heatwaves. These can cause changes in the growth and distribution of plants and animals, and coral **bleaching** on the Great Barrier Reef and Western Australian reefs.
Land and marine fauna ______________ (3) (*force*) to **migrate** away from areas that have become too warm, towards cooler places. This can cause an invasion by new species and the extinction of some existing ones that have nowhere to migrate to. In the last forty years, wildfires have become more frequent and larger areas ______________ (4) (*affect*).
The Great Barrier Reef is the largest coral reef in the world and the only living thing that ______________ (5) (*can + see*) from space. It is a system of about 3,000 individual reefs and 900 coral islands and it ______________ (6) (*can + compare*) to an underwater rainforest.
The Great Barrier Reef ______________ (7) (*critically affect*) by the increase in sea temperatures and CO_2 levels, and many of the species that live there ______________ (8) (*endanger*) by the declining health of the reef.
Kangaroo Island lies south-west of Adelaide and is home to some of Australia's most **iconic** wildlife species like koalas and platypuses. In the bushfires of 2019/2020, 46% of the island ______________ (9) (*burn*). The summer bushfires were the largest in the island's recorded history. 90% of native **habitat** ______________ (10) (*lose*) and thousands of animals ______________ (11) (*kill*).
Fraser Island ______________ (12) (*also know*) by its Aboriginal name, 'K'gari'. It is the world's largest sand dune island, with cliffs, unusual lakes and unique **ecosystems**. In 2020, an illegal beach campfire burnt this UNESCO World Heritage site. Since 1981, domestic dogs ______________ (13) (*ban*) from Fraser Island, as the pure genes of the wild dingoes that live there have high preservation value. There is great concern that many dingoes ______________ (14) (*injure*) or killed by the fire.

b Complete the article with the passive form of the verbs in brackets.

c Match the words in **bold** to these definitions.

1 the place where a plant or animal naturally lives: ______________
2 gradually losing colour: ______________
3 to move from one region or place to another: ______________
4 a community of organisms and its enviroment: ______________
5 famous and believed to represent a particular idea: ______________

21 **Why is Australia a global leader in wildlife extinctions?** Read the article and write the letters A – L for the phrases in the correct place.

A Australia's flora
B endemic species
C hectares of bushland
D Recent catastrophes
E threatened species and ecosystems
F flora and fauna species
G the federal government
H critically endangered across the continent
I threatened species towards extinction
J rapid urban and agricultural expansion
K The extinction of thirteen endemic species
L Environment Protection and Biodiversity Conservation

Plant and animal species in Australia are becoming extinct. […] Since colonization, about 100 of Australia's unique ______ (1) have been wiped off the planet. […] After […] Indonesia, Australia has the second-largest number of ______ (2) – plants and animals found nowhere else in the world. […]

Since federal laws were introduced in 1999, the list of ______ (3) has grown by more than a third – from 1,483 to 1,974. […] ______ (4) has officially been acknowledged by the Australian government, including twelve mammals and the first reptile which is known to have been lost since European colonization. […]

As well as some animal species, ______ (5) is under severe pressure: 37 species have been declared extinct. […] There are 1,336 species […] listed as threatened, including 191 that are ______ (6). […] The continent's […] wave of extinctions surged initially due to ______ (7) for the […] wool industry as well as the introduction of domestic cats, rabbits and foxes. […] Australia's rate of extinctions is expected to continue […] ______ (8) have caused significant damage. The Black Summer fires […] killed billions of animals, burnt 10 million ______ (9), and pushed ______ (10). […] While state laws had dealt with protecting threatened species, it wasn't until 1999 that ______ (11) became involved, with the ______ (12) (EPBC) Act. […]

Adapted from: www.smh.com.au and www.theguardian.com

22 LISTENING FOCUS: Youth climate network

7 **a** Ricky Bates and his friend Olivia are members of AYCC. Listen to the first part of the interview and do the tasks.

1 Explain what Seed Mob is.

____

____

____.

2 Explain what AYCC stands for and what they do.

____

____

____.

3 Describe Australia's situation in relation to greenhouse emissions.

____

____

____.

4 Explain the relationship between climate change and wildfires in Australia.

____

____

____.

8 **b** Listen to the second part of the interview and complete the sentences.

1 The climate crisis is unjust because ______________________________

____.

2 The most affected are ______________________________ because

____.

3 The cause of this situation is ______________________________

____.

4 In Australia, Aborigines and Torres Islands people ______________________________

____.

5 In a world based on climate justice, there would be ______________________________

____.

A New Zealand visit

23 A conversation about Kerikeri

a Jason and Paige are talking after lunch. Listen to their conversation, then describe what these expressions mean.

1 Pākehā ______
2 Kerikeri ______
3 Tecaddiecaddie ______
4 Aotearoa ______

b Outline why Kerikeri is called the 'Cradle of the Nation'.

______

______

c Summarize the early history of New Zealand. Use these numbers to help you. Write your summary in your exercise book (100 words).

1,000 400
1642 1769

24 Questions. Turn some of the questions that Paige and Jason asked into reported speech.

1 *Have you got many followers?* Paige wanted to know ______.

2 *Would you like to tell me about Christchurch for my blog?* Jason asked her ______.

3 *Can you tell me about Kerikeri?* Jason asked her ______.

4 *Where's Kerikeri?* Jason wanted to know ______.

5 *What does Kerikeri mean?* He asked her ______.

25 What Jason told Ricky. Ricky asked Jason about his conversation with Paige. Write how Jason reported what they said in your exercise book.

1 I think my aunt would be the best person for that.
2 I came here not long ago to live with my aunt.
3 Tell me something about the history of the city.
4 It is actually a town with fewer than 8000 inhabitants, but it's an important place.

26 **Kiwis and Aussies**

a Complete the text about the relationship between Australia and New Zealand with the correct form of the verbs in brackets and the missing prepositions.

Trans-Tasman ties

It ______________ (1) (*say*) that it is difficult to tell the difference ____________ (2) a Kiwi and an Aussie although it's different ________ (3) them. New Zealand and Australia have a lot ________ (4) common. They share a British colonial past, their recent history, largely similar varieties ________ (5) the English language, their isolation ________ (6) the rest of the world, businesses, institutions, and family ties. ________ (7) 1901, New Zealand was one of the seven UK colonies ________ (8) Australasia.

When Australia became a federation, New Zealand ____________________ (9) (*invite*) to become one of the states of the new Commonwealth of Australia. ____________ (10) much debate, it ________________________ (11) (*decide*) that New Zealand would remain independent.

However, the Australian constitution ____________________ (12) (*write*) to allow New Zealand to join as part of Australia ________ (13) any time if they wanted. There is a great rivalry that Aussies and Kiwis love to show. But it _________________ (14) (*root*) in their admiration of each other, in true ANZAC spirit.

But what is the ANZAC spirit? The ANZAC (Australian and New Zealand Army Corps) spirit refers to the bravery which the soldiers showed ________ (15) the battlefields of World War I. ANZAC Day ____________________________ (16) (*celebrate*) ________ (17) both countries on 25th April.

Several significant agreements, which ________________________ (18) (*sign*) since 1973, have brought New Zealand and Australia much closer, and a large number of political and governmental institutions _______________________ (19) (*now share*) by both.

b Find the following words in the text and write a definition in your own words.

1 recent: ______________________________

2 family ties: ______________________________

3 rivalry: ______________________________

4 battlefields: ______________________________

»» **c** Explain what you think *trans-Tasman* means. Write about 50 words in your exercise book.

Practice: Land of the Long White Cloud

27 The *haka*

10 a New Zealand's national rugby team, the All Blacks, is famous for performing the *haka*. Jason is asking Tai about it. Listen and tick (✓) what they talk about.

- ☐ 1 Jason's blog
- ☐ 2 Who reads the blog
- ☐ 3 What *haka* is
- ☐ 4 How the first *haka* was performed
- ☐ 5 When the first *haka* was performed
- ☐ 6 The legend of *haka*
- ☐ 7 The battles of *haka* warriors
- ☐ 8 When *haka* are performed
- ☐ 9 The types of *haka*
- ☐ 10 Who can perform *haka*

b Explain who these are and how they are related to *haka*.

1 Tama-nui-te-ra ______________________

2 Hine-raumati ______________________

3 Tane-rore ______________________

10 **c** Listen again and decide whether these statements are true or false. Correct the false ones.

		True	False
1	A haka was originally a war dance performed to frighten the enemy.	☐	☐
2	Nowadays, it is only performed before rugby matches.	☐	☐
3	There is only one way to perform haka.	☐	☐
4	Only men can perform the haka.	☐	☐

28 What did they say?

10 Ricky wants to find out more about Jason's conversation with Tai. These are the questions he asked Jason. Listen again and report Jason's answers.

1 How did Tai know about your blog?

He said ______________________.

2 What did Paige say about your blogpost? Did she like it?

Yes, she told me ______________________.

3 What did he say about the words of the *haka*?

He explained ______________________.

4 How did Tai react when you asked if you could upload the conversation to your blog?

He just laughed and said ______________________.

29 Maori culture

a Jason has found information about Maori culture for his blog. Complete it with the words and phrases from the box.

after that ■ founding constitutional document ■ however (2x) ■ increased focus on biculturalism ■ official languages ■ strong influence on all aspects ■ the indigenous people ■ therefore ■ undergoing a revival ■ which means 'treasure'

There are three ______________________ (1) in New Zealand: English, *Te Reo* Maori and New Zealand Sign Language. English is the main language; ______________________ (2), a recent survey by the New Zealand government found that about 130,000 people speak *Te Reo* Maori in New Zealand. This is around 4% of the population, making it the second most frequently-spoken language in the country. *Te Reo* Maori is considered a national taonga, ______________________ (3), and it is ______________________ (4): there are Maori language schools, a Maori language television station and a Maori Language Week.
Maori culture has a ______________________ (5) of life in the community from cuisine to family, social customs and language. Maori are the *tangata whenua*, ______________________ (6) of New Zealand. They arrived in New Zealand more than 1,000 years ago from their mythical Polynesian homeland of Hawaiki. In 1840, Maori Chiefs and representatives of the British crown signed the Treaty of Waitangi, New Zealand's ______________________ (7), which gave Maori people full rights and protection as British subjects. ______________________ (8), the British population quickly grew larger than the Maori population. British culture was dominant in New Zealand and, ______________________ (9), Maori had to adapt to it. ______________________ (10), Maori culture has experienced a comeback since the 1980s and there has been an ______________________ (11), which is based on the partnership established by the Treaty of Waitangi.

b Read Jason's article again and find four collective nouns.

____

Then write the collective noun for these definitions:

1 a group of people who sing together: ______________________
2 a group of people who work together, especially on a ship or a plane: ______________________
3 a group of people in a trial who decide if a person is guilty or not guilty: ______________________

30 READING FOCUS: New Zealand and climate change

a Ricky is concerned about climate change and does some research about New Zealand. Read the article and write a heading for each section.

A ______________________________

Climate change is one of the biggest issues facing our planet. People, species and our environment are at risk as carbon pollution is having negative impacts worldwide. Although New Zealand is a small country, we are one of the 30 biggest emitters per capita in the world and our emissions are growing. New Zealanders have big carbon footprints as each of us emits over 16 tonnes of greenhouse gases per year, which is more than the average European. In a ranking of 43 industrialized countries, New Zealand is one of twelve countries whose net emissions increased between 1990 and 2018.

B ______________________________

The temperature in the country has risen 0.9˚C over the last 100 years and this has already had an effect. The South Island glaciers are retreating and the volume of ice in the Southern Alps has decreased by 11% in the past 30 years. In the past 100 years, the sea level has risen by 16 cm on average across New Zealand's four major ports, the weather is getting warmer and, as a result, there are fewer frosts.

C ______________________________

The future looks grim. Temperatures will continue to rise, which will bring more droughts, erosion and flooding of coastal areas. The introduction of new pests and diseases will affect animal and human health and agriculture. It will also cause a serious decline in indigenous biodiversity. Water demand will increase during dry summers, and lower rainfall will reduce groundwater supplies. Campsites along one of New Zealand's walking tracks in the Abel Tasman National Park will be forced to move to higher ground, and a number of conservation areas are at risk from rising sea levels. If they rise between 0.5 to 1 metre by 2100 as predicted, the waves will destroy both natural and built defences, flooding land and waterways. Some councils are expecting an increase in the sea level of at least 50 cm which will seriously affect urban planning, for example, where to build new houses or how to dispose of waste. Wellington and Christchurch have already developed a plan to tackle the effects of climate change.

D ______________________________

We will face a significant climate impact unless we change to a 100% renewable energy future. The government has declared a climate emergency and has committed to becoming carbon-neutral. They will buy only electric or hybrid vehicles and coal-fired boilers will be phased out. Parliament has also passed the Zero Carbon Act 2019, which commits New Zealand to reducing emissions and which makes us one of the few countries to have a zero-emissions goal written into law.

b Now do these tasks in your exercise book.

1. Describe the consequences of higher temperatures in New Zealand.
2. Explain the importance of the Zero Carbon Act 2019.

Write an informative text

31 **Choose your topic.** Choose a topic, do some research and make notes.

- The unique bird species of New Zealand
- Government plans to make New Zealand carbon neutral ahead of the 2050 target
- New Zealand's 'School Strike 4 Climate' movement
- New Zealand as a filming location

Useful tips:
- Use various sources and check whether they are reliable.
- Skim the information you find and choose what is most relevant.
- Look up unknown words.
- Always cite your sources when you use other people's information.

32 **Write a draft.** Organize your notes in the three sections below, then write your first draft.

- Paragraph 1: Introduction
- Paragraphs 2 – 4: Descriptions, causes and effects, problems, consequences, what is being done, reasons, etc.
- Paragraph 5: Conclusion

Useful tips:
- Use a good (online) dictionary.
- Use a personal, conversational style.
- Use adjectives and adverbs to make your text more interesting.
- Use linking words and phrases to connect ideas and paragraphs.
- If necessary, include quotes from people involved.
- Check for correct spelling and grammar.

33 **Finish your text.** Write the final version. When you are happy with the corrections and changes, write the final draft of your text. Add photographs to make it more attractive.

Mediation

34 Australia in 100 days

a You and your classmates have been asked to present a film about a different country in class. You chose *Australia in 100 days*. Prepare a presentation in English in which you talk about how the film was made, what it is about and how it differs from other documentaries about Australia. Make notes (100 words).

Australien in 100 Tagen

Die unabhängigen Filmemacher Silke Schranz und Christian Wüstenberg waren 100 Tage mit dem Camper auf dem fünften Kontinent unterwegs. Ohne Kommerzbrille auf der Nase zeigen sie in sagenhaft schönen Bildern, was sie dort unglaublich spannend, beeindruckend und exotisch fanden. *Australien in 100 Tagen* ist ein Real-Roadmovie völlig ohne Pathos.

Viele Deutsche träumen von einem Urlaub in Australien. Das Problem dabei: Das Land ist riesengroß. Nach europäischem Maßstab reicht es von Lissabon bis Moskau oder von Nordnorwegen bis zur Türkei. Schon für An- und Abreise gehen vier Urlaubstage drauf. Also wohin soll die Reise gehen, wenn man nur zwei bis drei Wochen Zeit hat? Die Filmemacher Silke Schranz und Christian Wüstenberg sind 22 000 Kilometer um den ganzen Kontinent gereist, haben jeden Tag mit der Kamera dokumentiert und geben einen umfassenden Einblick in alle Regionen Australiens.

Der Unterschied zu normalen Dokus über andere Länder ist, dass *Australien in 100 Tagen* völlig ohne Pathos auskommt und dass die Filmemacher erzählen, als würden sie mit Freunden am Küchentisch sitzen und von ihren Erlebnissen berichten. Die filmische Reise beginnt in Perth, geht die einsame Westküste hoch bis Darwin, über Alice Springs im Roten Zentrum bis ins tropische Cairns und von dort Richtung Süden über Sydney und Melbourne bis nach Adelaide. Sogar einen Abstecher ins ursprüngliche Tasmanien haben die beiden gemacht. Entstanden ist eine gut gelaunte Mischung aus persönlichen Erlebnissen, Naturdoku und Reiseführer.

„Wir haben das Ganze als Kinofilm konzipiert, weil die Schönheit der Natur nur auf der großen Leinwand ihre volle Wirkung entfalten kann. Das Kino macht Australien zu einem Naturereignis“, sagt Christian Wüstenberg. „Wir hatten so viele tolle Erlebnisse, wir sind mit Riesenschildkröten geschwommen, haben den höchsten Berg Australiens bestiegen, sind im Wasserflugzeug zum weißesten Strand der Welt geflogen und haben im Outback nach Saphiren geschürft. Wirklich jeder kann das, was wir gemacht haben auch erleben und die Route aus dem Film direkt nachreisen.“ Damit die Zuschauer die Tipps auch Schwarz auf Weiß haben, ist im Mana-Verlag das Buch zum Film *Australien in 100 Tagen* erschienen.

Taken from: www.comfilm.de

b You ask a friend to watch *Australia in 100 days* in the cinema with you. Your friend wants to know if the film is worth watching and you find a review online. Write an email to your friend (80 words) and explain what the review says.

Marc, 30 years, lives in Sydney

Last week I saw the movie *Australia in 100 days* because my friend Tony had heard about it. Before I watched the film, I had doubts that Germans could make an authentic film about our continent. What can I say? I must admit that I enjoyed watching this documentary, which shows some positive and negative aspects of our country. The fact that English is only a second language for the presenter does not disturb in the least. The photography is great, and I was shown spots in Australia that I hadn't heard of before, for example in Tasmania. The honesty with which the film-makers show Australia and its inhabitants sometimes made me smile.

My review

1 About persuasive language

a

1 ages
2 rather
3 simply
4 heaps of / loads of
5 amazing / awesome
6 loads of / heaps of
7 yummy
8 awesome / amazing
9 uniquely
10 blazing

b

1 out
2 to
3 up
4 round
5 on
6 down
7 after
8 up
9 off
10 up

2 About Australian history

1 were
2 began
3 had been living
4 had not taken part in
5 had initially joined
6 reached
7 had been travelling
8 was not
9 left
10 did not have
11 got back
12 had already died
13 returned
14 had already left
15 had also died

3 About the climate

1 have been wiped out
2 can only be found
3 are shown
4 have been cut down
5 should not be ignored
6 has to be made clear
7 are killed
8 must be taken
9 is done
10 will be lost

4 About a travel experience

a

1 asked
2 told
3 wanted to know
4 described
5 explained
6 said

b

7 were
8 that week
9 met up
10 the following month
11 would be able to
12 heard
13 would want
14 had never been
15 there

New Directions

1 **After high school.** Read this article about career paths from an online teen magazine and fill the gaps with the *to*-infinitive or gerund of the verms in brackets. Sometimes both forms are possible.

What to do after school?

What can you imagine ____________________ (1) (*do*) after school? Maybe you'd like ____________________ (2) (*start*) at university right away. Before deciding, some students like ____________________ (3) (*work*) in gig jobs for a while to earn some money. Many of them are looking forward to ____________________ (4) (*spend*) the money on travelling before they start ____________________ (5) (*study*) or decide ____________________ (6) (*work*). And what about you? Are you interested in ____________________ (7) (*meet*) people from other cultures? Then how about a gap year? Try ____________________ (8) (*research*) different options on the internet. Remember ____________________ (9) (*sign up*) for newsletters from charitable organizations which offer opportunities to work abroad. If you prefer ____________________ (10) (*stay*) at home but are sure that you really don't want ____________________ (11) (*study*), you should consider ____________________ (12) (*look at*) vocational schools. They offer some great courses. Whatever you plan ____________________ (13) (*do*) when you leave school, don't forget ____________________ (14) (*ask*) your peers and advisors for advice.

2 **What the future holds.** A group of students are talking about their plans for the future. Read their conversation and complete it with the best future form of the verbs in brackets.

Emilia: Have you decided what you ____________________ (1) (*do*) after school?

Liam: Yes, I have. I ____________________ (2) (*study*) economics and maybe I ____________________ (3) (*also take*) a writing course. When I graduate, I think I ____________________ (4) (*try*) to get an internship with a newspaper and maybe I ____________________ (5) (*end up*) working for a news media company. And you?

Emilia: I want to be an aerospace engineer. Many people think it's not a career for girls but I ____________________ (6) (*definitely do*) it.

continued on next page

Liam Good for you!

Emilia The course ____________________ (7) (*begin*) next September and, by the time I turn 30, I ________________________ (8) (*sign*) a contract with NASA!

Sophia I ________________________ (9) (*do*) an internship with a law firm next term. It ________________________ (10) (*start*) at the beginning of July and I think it ________________________________ (11) (*help*) me to decide. And you, Anton?

Anton I ________________________ (12) (*join*) the creative writing club next term and I ________________________ (13) (*apply*) for the Performing Arts School. I hope my dream to be an actor ________________________ (14) (*come*) true!

3 The future of work

11 **a** A consultant is giving a talk about young people and the future of work. Listen to the first part and decide if the sentences are true or false. Correct the false sentences.

		True	False
1	The results of the study do not throw a positive light on education systems.	☐	☐
2	They also show that the world of work is becoming increasingly inclusive.	☐	☐
3	Young people feel that they are not completely aware of the challenges the world of work poses.	☐	☐
4	On the whole, young people think that technology will have a great impact on employment = generating new jobs.	☐	☐
5	Just under 50% of young people think that they won't be able to get a permanent, full-time job because of digital technology.	☐	☐
6	More than 50% of young people don't think they will be able to find the jobs they really want.	☐	☐

____

____

____

12 **b** Listen to the second part and choose the correct ending (A–E) for sentences 1–5.

1 In the UK, children aged between seven and eleven and between ages 17 and 18
2 The most popular careers are
3 The problem with this choice of career is
4 The problem teenagers face is
5 The consultant suggests that one way of helping young people prepare for the world of work is to

A get employers participating at a much earlier stage in a student's education.
B in culture, media and sport occupations.
C choose similar types of jobs.
D that there is nothing in common between their career ambitions and projected labour market demand.
E that they know little about the job opportunities and career paths available, so make uninformed decisions.

Practice: A work opportunity

4 LISTENING FOCUS: Bernardine's adventure

a Listen to the interview and complete the sentences.

13

1 After finishing school, Bernardine wanted the chance ______________________________.

2 She decided ______________________________.

3 She asked her parents ______________________________.

4 With her jobs she managed ______________________________.

5 She spent a whole year ______________________________.

14

b Listen to the second part and complete the summary with the letters A – J for the phrases below. Note down the changes Bernardine experienced during her journey.

A had collected
B in travel books
C internship successfully
D offered her a job
E staying in Asia
F 30 notebooks (full of notes and pictures)
G becoming a travel journalist
H she would go to law school
I the quality of her work
J to record her experiences

There was a point in her journey when Bernardine considered _____ (1) but she couldn't afford to travel for much longer without finding a job. Before leaving, she had done a photojournalism internship because she wanted _____ (2) in the countries she visited. By the time she returned, she _____ (3) videos, photos and _____ (4). She completed her _____ (5) and one of her 'bosses', who was the project manager of a publishing company which specializes _____ (6), said he was impressed by _____ (7) and _____ (8). Bernardine had never thought about _____ (9) because she had always thought _____ (10).

14

c Listen to the second part again and find expressions that mean the same as the following:

1 to have enough money to be able to pay for sth.: ______________________

2 to tell the end of a story without giving details: ______________________

3 to happen in a certain way or have an unexpected result: ______________________

4 to feel worried about sth. that might have happened: ______________________

d What do you think about Bernardine's journey and decision? What are the pros and cons? Write about 80 words in your exercise book.

5 Looking for a job

a Read the job adverts and complete them with the best future form of the verbs in brackets.

A

IT Recruitment Officer

We are looking for recent graduates who want to work in the digital industry. After your training, you ______________________ (1) (*work*) with recruiters to create job descriptions. You ______________________ (2) (*advertise*) jobs and updating the database. You must be able to work under pressure and be very self-motivated. These qualities ______________________ (3) (*help*) you progress within the company. Competitive salary plus commission. Part-time positions available.

B

Insurance Telesales

Are you over 18 years old and available between January and March next year? This three-month fixed-term role involves calling customers and asking them if they ______________________ (4) (*renew*) their policy. The hours of work are 8.45 a.m. until 5 p.m. Monday to Friday. We are looking for someone with good computer skills. No previous sales experience necessary. Two-week in-house training course provided. You ______________________ (5) (*acquire*) all the necessary skills to work with us by the end of your training and ______________________ (6) (*be able to*) work independently.

C

Data Analyst

As a Data Analyst you ______________________ (7) (*join*) a team that analyses research data. This is an ideal position for recent graduates or advanced students of Economics, Marketing or Finance. Both part-time and full-time positions offered. If your application is successful, you ______________________ (8) (*do*) a three-week entry training course. The course ______________________ (9) (*start*) on 1st September. Competitive salary and annual bonus. Both part-time and full-time positions offered.

D

Project Assistant

You ______________________ (10) (*work*) closely with the Project Manager's team. You ______________________ (11) (*do*) property surveys. You ______________________ (12) (*also attend*) meetings to ensure work is done properly. You must have initiative, as you ______________________ (13) (*have to*) work on your own. Candidates should be graduates from a construction-related career. Previous experience is not essential.

b Read the job adverts again – if necessary check the meanings of unknown words. Then answer the questions. Sometimes there is more than one correct answer. Which job …

1 is part-time? ________________

2 requires no previous experience? ________________

3 gives employees the opportunity to earn more by making sales? ________________

4 requires experience in the building industry? ________________

5 is temporary? ________________

6 offers training? ________________

c Some candidates applied for the jobs and have had interviews. Read what the interviewers said and choose the correct future form. Then decide which job each interviewer is talking about.

Interviewer 1 You **will have attended / will attend** (1) meetings with teams on construction sites in different parts of the country. You **will get / are going to get** (2) a fixed amount of money each month to cover your expenses.

Job: ________________________________

Interviewer 2 By the end of the year, your manager **will be writing / will have written** (3) reports on your work which **will help / are going to help** (4) you learn what your strengths and weaknesses are. We **will take / are going to take** (5) them into account to decide on your end-of-year bonus.

Job: ________________________________

Interviewer 3 The training course you **will be doing / will have done** (6) with us **is giving / will give** (7) you all the tools that you need to do the job successfully. The two-week course **starts / is going to start** (8) at 9 a.m. every day.

Job: ________________________________

Interviewer 4 I am sure you **make / will make** (9) good progress because you are highly motivated. By the time you have been working with us for about five years, you **are going to receive / will have received** (10) promotion as well as a salary increase.

Job: ________________________________

»» **d** Explain which job you would like to apply for and why. Which one would you never consider applying for? Give reasons for your answers. Write about 50 words in your exercise book.

Applying for a job

6 A cover letter

a A popular influencer is giving advice about how to write a good cover letter. Listen and make a list of dos and don'ts in a table. Then check with a partner.

b Listen again and decide if the following sentences are true or false. Correct the false ones in your exercise book.

		True	False
1	You may get a job interview or have your CV ignored depending on how good your cover letter is.	☐	☐
2	When you write a cover letter, you should explain why you are interested in the company or organization.	☐	☐
3	In a good cover letter, you should explain extensively what you have done in your life.	☐	☐
4	It's a good idea to include details about your personal life so that the interviewer knows what sort of person you are.	☐	☐
5	Use the cover letter to ask relevant questions about the salary, working conditions, holidays, etc.	☐	☐

7 Useful advice.
Rewrite these sentences in your exercise book using the modal verbs in brackets.

1 Your cover letter will probably decide if you get an interview or not. (*may*)

2 Include specific information on why you are a good match for the job. (*must*)

3 Writing a long cover letter is out of the question. (*mustn't*)

4 It is not necessary to include personal or family details in your cover letter. (*not have to*)

8 Expressing feelings.
Complete the influencer's advice with these sentence adverbs.

additionally ■ basically ■ naturally ■ normally ■ theoretically

1 ____________________, your cover letter will make the difference between getting a job interview or having your CV ignored.

2 ____________________, your letter should give information about your suitability for the position.

3 ____________________, the letter shouldn't repeat what's on your CV.

4 ____________________, it shouldn't be too long.

5 ____________________, you should avoid asking about salary in your letter.

9 **Giving feedback.** Three students have written cover letters applying for a job. Choose one of the letters and give the student feedback on style, and correct any mistakes. Use the modal verbs from the box. Write about 80 words in your exercise book.

could ■ may ■ might ■ must ■ need ■ should

A

Shop assistant

To whom it may concern:

I read your ad for the assistant position and would like to apply. As my CV shows, I have a lot of great experience that you can use. And, IMHO, this job is exactly what I want!!!

Please review my CV and call me soon to schedule an interview. I am so eager to meet you.

Hope to CU soon!!!

Sincerely,

Debbie Reynolds

B

Cashier

Dear Mr Smith,

Hope you are having a good day. I want to help make it beter by telling you all the reasons I am exactly right for the role of cashier:

- I have always dreamd about working for your company.
- The comuting distance is great.
- The salary is exactly what I've been looking for.
- This is exactly what I need for this summer.

Please call me on 555-345-1001 so we can explore this further. I look forward to hearing from you soon.

Sincerely,

Jake

C

Summer Camp environmental projects coordinator

Dear Mister Ryan Fellows,

I am applying for the environmental projects coordinator position. I was born to get this job. Please let me explain why I am such a good match. As a little girl, my two brothers and I used to go camping with my parents. We were taught to respect nature, and to this day theres nothing I love more than being outdoors. I even joined the girl scouts when I was a kid, so I could improve my camping skills. I am proud to say that I earned many badges.

I have spent the last two years of my life preparing my A-levels. I did well and got accepted by the uni I wanted, but I still feel like something is missing.

Today, I saw the listing for your job and knew I had to write to you. Since I read about your job, it's all I can think about. I really hope you are willing to give me a chance.

Please consider me seriously. I know I can do the job, and what I don't know yet I will learn quickly. Scout's honour!

Hopefully,

Mariah Vermont

Practice: Presenting your best self

10 Job ads

a Read the job ads and decide which of the jobs you would be most interested in applying for. Then make some notes about your skills, strengths, interests and qualifications.

A

Dog walker
Love dogs? Your neighbourhood canine friends need exercise, and their owners aren't always available to take them out for a stroll. That's where you come in.

Requirements: A love for pups is obvious, but you'll also likely need to be able to commit to a daily or weekly schedule.
Pay: €11 per hour

B

Childcare worker
Building positive learning outcomes and life skills with children and students.
Requirements: Hard-working, responsible student with experience taking care of young children.
Key skills include:
- Spanish (intermediate) and French (beginner)
- First Aid, CPR, AED certifications

Pay: €18 per hour

C

Lifeguard
You'll be keeping watch over the pool, the lake, or the ocean to make sure everyone is safe and out of danger. It's one of the most popular jobs for teens out there.

Requirements: Lifeguard / CPR certification, as well as a watchful eye. The organization will supply this training.
Pay: €12 per hour

D

Camp counsellor
There are many kinds of camps – wilderness camps, sports camps, academic camps – but in general, counsellors help plan and lead fun activities with groups of kids.

Requirements: You should have an interest in working with groups of children and have a passion for whatever subject you're teaching.
Pay: €12 per hour

15 **b** Write your CV and a cover letter on a separate piece of paper in an appropriate form. If necessary, listen again to the tips from track 15 on page 38. Then swap with a partner and give each other feedback.

11 READING FOCUS: The glass ceiling

a Before you read the text opposite, speculate what the term 'glass ceiling' means. Choose one of the options below. Then read the first two paragraphs of the article and check your answer.

☐ 1 the barriers which prevent women entering certain occupations
☐ 2 the different salaries for men and women
☐ 3 the barriers which prevent women moving from one company to another
☐ 4 the difficulties women face when trying to climb up the job ladder

The Glass Ceiling

The future of work debate has failed to analyse gender difference or to understand the hopes and fears of women workers for their own future of work. Including women's voices in this debate is vital because women make up 40% of the global labour force and their current experience is marked by gaps and traps in access to good jobs, pay outcomes and many other indicators when compared to men. A report about women in leadership positions reveals that only 24% of CEOs are women and they earn 87.9 % as much as male CEOs. They work the same amount of time, their education is equal to or higher than their male counterparts, and their leadership skills are excellent. ______ (1)

The glass ceiling is an invisible barrier between women and top executive positions which prevents them from reaching the highest levels of the business world. ______ (2)

Although much has improved since the term was first used back in the 1970s, because of the glass ceiling, educated and highly experienced women aren't equally represented in many professional groups and industries, which are still considered to be male-dominated. However, women are twice as likely to work in the tourism industry than in other sectors. Tourism companies would rather employ women than men because of their ability to empathize, their kindness, and so-called maternal instinct. ______ (3)

______ (4) Minority women in white-majority countries often find it most difficult to break the glass ceiling because they are at the intersection of two historically marginalized groups: women and people of colour. It's fair to claim that the world of work is changing, and women are becoming much more recognized than they used to be. ______ (5) Girls should speak up in class. They shouldn't allow anyone to limit what they want to achieve by assuming that they can't. Women should speak up in the workplace, and when an opportunity for a promotion comes up at work, they must ask for it. ______ (6)

b Now read the rest of the text and choose the best photo to illustrate it.

A

B

C

c Read the complete article again and put the following parts in the correct place. Then discuss your results with a partner.

A Angela Merkel, Jacinda Ardern and Kamala Harris have experience of leading their countries. What is stopping you from leading a company or your country in the future?

B But we need to continue challenging the belief that women can't be executives or hold high-ranking positions.

C Men apparently dominate the world of work and, almost inevitably, 'the glass ceiling' appears above a female's head.

D Nevertheless, the report also says that even though women are well represented, they tend to work at a service rather than a decision-making level.

E The glass ceiling is different from the gender pay gap, which is the fact that women on average earn 20 % less than men for the same work.

F Women and minorities are the ones who suffer the consequences of the glass ceiling.

d Decide if these sentences are true, false or not in the text (NT). Correct the false ones.

		True	False	NT
1	Although women work the same number of hours as men, and their education and leadership skills are the same, they earn less and find it harder to get top management positions.	☐	☐	☐
2	The gender pay gap, which is also known as the glass ceiling, is the difference in average earnings between women and men.	☐	☐	☐
3	There are certain professions, such as the tourism industry that continue being mostly dominated by men.	☐	☐	☐
4	Women and minorities suffer the glass ceiling the most.	☐	☐	☐
5	The situation hasn't changed since the 1970s and it doesn't look like it's going to change any time soon.	☐	☐	☐
6	Women in government leadership positions have become normal.	☐	☐	☐

12 **Career growth.** Read a consultant's advice and complete it with the correct verbs.

Many areas of industry have seen significant changes. However, it **must be said / should say** (1) that, unfortunately, there is still room for improvement. It **can be / may be** (2) hard to believe, but on average, for every 100 men who are promoted to managerial positions, only 72 women get promoted and hired.
So what **can / need** (3) you do to stand out from the crowd? First, you **need / should** (4) consider taking development courses to further your education. However, this course of action **may not / must not** (5) be an option for some women who are expected to look after the family as well as advancing their career.
Nowadays, thanks to online programmes, many women **are able to / have to** (6) meet their educational goals. You **should also ask / don't have to ask** (7) teammates or managers for feedback outside of the review process. This **may / must** (8) help you find out which additional skills you **need / should** (9) to learn. You **should / need** (10) look for a mentor who can support your career goals.

Communicate effectively in an interview

13 Identify communication strategies

16 **a** Listen to three mini dialogues and identify which communication strategies the speakers use. Give examples from the dialogues.

- Asking for repetition: ______________________________
- Asking for clarification: ______________________________
- Making time to think: ______________________________

b Write your own mini dialogue using communication strategies. Pick one of these situations and write at least two exchanges.

- Asking the way and not understanding the instruction.
- Turning down an invitation in a nice way.

14 Evaluating interviews

2 **a** Watch Gabriela's first job interview and take notes on these factors:

	Notes
Greeting	
Punctuality	
Posture	
Clothes	
Clear speech	
Asks for repetition/ clarification	
General attitude	

3 **b** Now watch the second video. What did Gabriela do better? Make some notes.

c Choose one of the interviews and put yourself in the position of the hiring manager. Write a short report in your exercise book and say why you would or wouldn't hire Gabriela.

The changing world of work

15 How it used to be

a Complete this extract about what life was like for people who migrated from Europe to the US with the correct form of the verbs in brackets: simple past, past progressive or past perfect.

At the turn of the 20th century, many immigrants __________ (1) (*settle*) in the US, and by 1920, millions __________ (2) (*enter*) the country. They __________ (3) (*hope*) for a better life, but many were shocked because it was not what they __________ (4) (*expect*). People sometimes __________ (5) (*have to*) work 10 to 12 hours a day, seven days a week. Workers __________ (6) (*not have*) any job security, a retirement fund or compensation if they __________ (7) (*become*) sick or injured. People __________ (8) (*lose*) their jobs if they __________ (9) (*be*) too sick or injured to work. Employees __________ (10) (*not take*) lunch breaks, and they __________ (11) (*work*) non-stop. Many immigrant women and children __________ (12) (*also start*) working in factories. Life in the rural areas was not easy either. Many farm workers __________ (13) (*spend*) hours working outside in all seasons, exposed to extreme hot and cold weather. These poor working conditions __________ (14) (*lead*) to unrest and strikes. However, at the same time, this had a positive effect on the unions which then __________ (15) (*grow*) and became stronger.

b Now rewrite these sentences from the text using *used to / didn't use to* in your exercise book. Which of these sentences can you rewrite with *would*?

1 Working conditions were harsh with low wages and long working days.
2 Workers didn't have any job security.
3 People lost their jobs if they were too sick or injured to work.
4 Employees didn't take lunch breaks, and they worked non-stop.
5 Many farm workers spent hours working outside in all seasons.

16 **The life of a freelancer.** Read the interview and choose the correct forms.

I. Freelancing sounds like the perfect way of working. Nobody **lets / makes** (1) you do things you don't like want to do. That **lets / makes** (2) me think it must be wonderful!
F. Well, yes, freelancing **allows / lets** (3) you to choose your own working hours and organize your own daily routine. If you are a morning person, you can finish work early which **will let / will make** (4) you have more free time in the evening. But, of course, if you use normal 'office hours' to do chores, that can **let / make** (5) the day seem very long.
I. And being a freelancer **allows / lets** (6) you work from anywhere, doesn't it?
F. Sure, but don't forget the downsides. Freelancing **lets / makes** (7) some people take on too much work – you know there is the constant fear that work will 'dry up'.
I. OK, but surely it must **allow / let** (8) you have a better work-life balance.
F. Only if you don't **allow / make** (9) work to take up all your time. Not having a fixed schedule can **let / make** (10) 'work' and 'life' become blurred.

17 **How life changed.** Read about the impact of the Covid-19 pandemic. Complete the text with the letters A – H for the phrases below.

A have had their working hours reduced
B had their day changed
C had their meals delivered
D had their hours increased and their holidays cancelled
E had their office chair brought
F had their shopping done
G have their work corrected
H have your hair cut or coloured

During the lockdown caused by the Covid-19 pandemic, society experienced significant changes which impacted all areas of life. Schools were closed and students were taught online. Some teachers were very inventive, others struggled. In some cases, students couldn't ________ (1) as their schools were not equipped with the right technology. Parents of younger children ________ (2) completely. They had to help their children with schoolwork, which meant long night shifts to catch up with their own work, often at the kitchen table. The result for some was backache from hours sitting on an unsuitable chair. The lucky ones came up with a solution – they ________ (3) to their homes! Life was hard for older people, too, and many were very isolated. In some cities, elderly citizens ________ (4) by the city council because carers or family members were not allowed to do it for them. They also ________ (5) by neighbours or volunteers. You couldn't ________ (6) at the hairdresser's, so many people had to get used to a new look! And, on a more serious note, a lot of businesses had to close. Since 2020, many workers ________ (7) and many more have lost their jobs. Medical staff in hospitals were the real heroes – many ________ (8) in order to cope with the huge numbers of patients.

Practice: The wealth divide

18 **The Royal Family.** Read the introduction to an article about the British Royal Family and put the verbs in the correct tense. Use *used to* where appropriate.

Today's British Royal Family are very different than they ____________ (1) (*be*). They ____________ (2) (*follow*) a strict protocol but this ____________ (3) (*relax*) in recent years. In the past, British monarchs ____________ (4) (*not be allowed to*) marry a divorced person. This rule ____________ (5) (*change*) and, in 2005, Prince Charles, who ____________ (6) (*divorce*) Diana in 1996, ____________ (7) (*marry*) Camilla. Another change is who becomes the next king or queen. Sons ____________ (8) (*come*) before daughters, but in 2015, a new law ____________ (9) (*come*) into force which means Charlotte, Prince William's daughter, may one day become Queen. In the past, royals only ____________ (10) (*marry*) other royals. This tradition ____________ (11) (*change*), too, and both Prince William and Prince Harry ____________ (12) (*marry*) non-royals.

19 **Royal perks.** There are many things that the Royal Family don't have to worry about. Read the sentences and rewrite them with *have something done*.

1 The Treasury pays for the Queen's bills.
The Queen ____________________________.

2 The Sovereign Grant pays for the salaries of employees who work for the Royal Family.
Employees ____________________________.

3 The British government paid for the security at Prince William's wedding.
Prince William ____________________________.

4 A servant brings the Queen all the newspapers to her breakfast table every day.
The Queen ____________________________.

5 A nanny looked after the Queen's four children when they were small.
The Queen ____________________________.

20 **Protocol rules!** Protocol is important and the Royal Family are required to follow strict rules. Rewrite these rules using the expressions in brackets.

1 All his married life, Prince Philip had to walk behind the Queen, his wife. *(be required to)*

____.

2 Under no circumstances can a member of the Royal Family vote or express political opinions in public. *(be allowed to)*

____.

3 Members of the Royal Family should not show affection in public. *(be supposed to)*

____.

4 Members of the Royal Family should dress appropriately at all times. *(be required to)*

____.

5 You can't take a selfie with the monarch or ask for an autograph. *(be permitted to)*

____.

21 **Taking action**

17 **a** Nele and Luka are discussing Mary and Braeden, two young people who decided to take action to help others. Listen and do these tasks.

1 Complete the facts about Mary with numbers from the cloud. There are two you don't need.

a Mary started her idea of making and selling headbands when she was ______________.

b Her plan was to make enough money to pay for ______________ girl's schooling.

c Now, at the age of ______________ and thanks to her charity, ______________ girls are currently in school.

d This has been achieved by making and selling over ______________ headbands and other hair accessories.

1 12 53 10,000 16 35 100,000

2 Choose two sentences which best summarize what Braeden has done.

a His project aims to help unemployed people find work by helping them write letters.
b His project offers homeless people a bag containing healthy snacks, water and information about services which offer more help.
c His project aims to fight hunger by giving homeless people money to buy healthy food and water.
d He also organizes fundraising events to raise money to help fight hunger.
e He also organizes events with famous people like Michelle Obama.
f Michelle Obama has information about Braeden's project on her website.

18 **b** Listen to the second part of the discussion with Noah and do the tasks in your exercise book.

1 List the solutions Luka suggests.
2 Say what 'DoSomething.org' is.
3 Explain what 'Teens for Jeans' is.
4 Outline Nele's plan.
5 Explain what Noah suggests.

22 WRITING FOCUS: Young Minds activist

19 **a** Jason is a Young Minds activist. He's being interviewed on a youth TV programme about his work. Listen to the interview and make notes on the following:

1 Young Minds aims ____________________

____

____

2 What a Young Minds activist is (e.g. age, profile) ____________________

____

____

3 Jason's experience ____________________

____

____

4 Jason's brother ____________________

____

____

5 Activist activities ____________________

____

____

b Read about other ways of volunteering with Young Minds. Use the information in the interview and ads below to write a report in your exercise book (150 – 180 words).

Youth Panel

Interested in learning more about how a charity is run? Have an understanding of mental health and the issues affecting young people?

- Communicate with Senior Management Team and other departments across the organization
- Spread the word
- Help to change attitudes towards mental health
- Find the funds to help run the charity

People aged 14 – 25 living in the UK can apply.

Young Minds blog

Digital Writers Pool: You're sent an email every 2 – 4 weeks with blog topics to write about. All writers go by their first name, or are anonymous.

- Young people share their experiences and support others
- Turn real life experiences into positive change for children and young people's mental health
- Use your voice and tell your stories
- Each month different themes are covered: real life stories, tips and advice, recovery and reaching out for help

Aged under 18? Parent / Guardian must give consent.

An internship abroad

23 **Out of your comfort zone.** Nele's class is attending a talk about internships abroad. Read the information leaflet and underline examples of participle constructions.

Internships abroad

In a globalized world, experience gained by living and interning abroad is critical to help you build your career. Showing your willingness to step out of your comfort zone looks good on your CV. After completing an internship, your experience, skills and confidence will help you appear more competitive. When included on your CV, internships make you a more interesting candidate.
While finding out what you like and dislike is not always easy, going on an internship will help you when making decisions regarding which path you're interested in following. Having experienced real work situations, you'll see your strengths, which areas you might want to work on, and which are simply not for you.
'If asked about it as a Human Resources Manager, I can tell you that applying for a job is tough. Having work experience through internships makes you an interesting candidate, which increases your chances of getting a job. It also says a lot about you. Having taken the time to look and apply for an internship, shows your dedication.'
(Nathaniel Wilkins, HR Manager, Stirling & Associates)

24 **The internship process.** Rewrite the underlined parts using participle constructions.

1 After you have reviewed our offer, determine where and when you want to go.

____

______________________________.

2 If you're still undecided which location to choose, connect with our Relations Manager who will help you decide.

____

______________________________.

3 Before our Registration Officer admits you, he will ask you to submit other documents: CV, cover letter, school approval, transcript, and placement interest form.

____

______________________________.

4 The Internship Coordinator will discuss your career goals and interests. She will use the city you have chosen as a basis.

____

______________________________.

25 An internship in Costa Rica

20 **a** Noah's sister Fran went on an internship after graduating. Listen to her talking about it to Noah and his friend Nele and complete the sentences.

1 Fran didn't go on an internship ______________________

____

____.

2 She went because ____

____.

3 When she was at school, Fran ____

____.

4 Nele was excited because ____

____.

20 **b** Listen again. Outline the advice Fran gives Noah and Nele.

____

____

____

c These extracts are from the conversation. Rewrite the underlined parts without participles.

1 Okay, let's see. <u>If asked why I did it</u>, I'd say I'm not …

____.

2 <u>Having done a lot of campaigning</u> for environmental groups in Australia, …

____

____.

3 So, as I was saying, <u>knowing that an internship</u> would provide me with unique opportunities to work on sustainability or conservation projects, …

____

____.

4 <u>Having top marks in science</u>, I was accepted almost immediately.

____

____.

5 I worked with an organization in Costa Rica, <u>run by the Ministry of Environment and Energy</u>, doing a number of things.

____

____.

Practice: Closing the gender gap

26 Gender gap in education

a Read about the gender gap in education. Then find words to match the definitions below.

The aim of the programme which was launched (1) by UNESCO, UN Women, the UN Population Fund (UNFPA) and the World Bank is to empower young women through education. The programme, which was announced (2) by UNESCO Director General Irina Bokova, provides a collaborative effort to close the gender gap in education.
When she spoke (3) at the launch event, Irina Bokova said that an increase in the education of young women carries impact across generations. Among other things, education could reduce the number of women who are dying (4) in childbirth in sub-Saharan Africa by 70%, which would save (5) over 100,000 lives every year. We must ensure that every door to the education of girls and women remains open across the life cycle. This is crucial.
But education for girls is about more than access to school. Girls should feel safe in classrooms and they should also be supported in the subjects and careers they pursue. Barriers to girls' education vary among countries and communities. In countries which have been affected (6) by conflict, girls are more than twice as likely to be out of school than girls who live (7) in non-affected countries. Poor families often favour boys when they think about making an investment in education. To invest in girls' secondary education is one of the most transformative development strategies. If they are given (8) the same chances as boys, girls will have the same potential to succeed.

1 an event to celebrate or introduce something new: ____________________

2 to give someone official authority to do something: ____________________

3 to try to achieve an aim, a plan, an activity, etc.: ____________________

4 putting money, etc. into something to make a profit: ____________________

b Read the article again and shorten the underlined parts using participle constructions.

____

____

____

____

____

____

____

>>> **c** Look for information about the gender gap in education in Germany. Write 150 – 180 words in your exercise book using the article above as a model.

27 **My future.** Three young people are talking about their future. Replace the underlined words with the correct form of the phrasal verbs from the box. Write in your exercise book.

carry on ■ come up with ■ get round ■ point out ■ put off ■ set up ■ take part ■ take up ■ talk about ■ think about

Miri — I was really stressed out with the whole college application process, I was seriously considering (1) giving up on it altogether – or at least postponing it (2) till next year. Fortunately, I found a college that was the right fit for me and it turned into a great experience.

Josh — I've always had an interest in science, so I wanted to do (3) genetics at university. Some time ago, I participated (4) in a science fair. There were people from the college there. After they had attended my presentation, they suggested (5) a course of studies that would be perfect for me.

Dale — My parents have always wanted me to be a lawyer and they have explained (6) that I'd have a comparative advantage: the family firm! Last month, I arranged (7) appointments with a couple of universities to discuss (8) my options, but then I realized it is not what I want. I'm going to continue (9) looking. And in the meantime, I just have to persuade (10) my parents to let me take a gap year!

28 **SPEAKING FOCUS: Gender bias**

a If asked to draw or imagine a firefighter, a brain surgeon and a fighter plane pilot, what would you draw or imagine? Discuss with a partner.

b The same experiment was carried out with students in different countries. Describe what you think they drew.

____

____

____

4 **c** Watch a video recording of the experiment. Was your prediction correct? Make notes to summarize what the experiment shows. Talk about the video.

____

____

____

____

____

____

____

____

____

29 21 **Gender stereotypes.** Listen to a talent management expert. Decide if the following sentences are true or false and correct the false ones.

		True	False
1	The video was made with child actors and real teachers.	☐	☐
2	All the children drew men.	☐	☐
3	The teachers also worked as a firefighter, a pilot and a surgeon.	☐	☐
4	The experiment was carried out in 20 schools in the UK.	☐	☐
5	It showed that gender bias in children starts at an early age.	☐	☐
6	According to the results of the experiment, children are mostly influenced by their families.	☐	☐

____

____

____

____

30 **Comparing countries.** Discuss examples of gender bias in the English language and in German.

31 **Challenging the gender gap**

a Match the correct sentence endings to find out about a young entrepreneur who challenged the gender gap in business and education.

1 Avye Couloute started coding and attending …
2 Noticing that the majority of the workshop attendees were boys, …
3 GIC offers girls aged 10 to 14 opportunities …
4 Through her programme, she aims …
5 Avye also established a community interest company with her mother …
6 She has entered and won competitions …

A with the robots she designs and makes.
B she decided to set up Girls into Coding (GIC).
C which aims to ensure a higher participation of girls and women in STEM.
D to involve at least 1,000 girls each year.
E computing workshops from the age of 7.
F to explore coding, physical computing, robotics and 3D printing.

»» **b** Think about your personal interests and ambitions. What sort of business project would you like to start? Write down your ideas. Consider what you would need to do, who could help you and who would benefit from your project. Prepare a presentation for your class.

Role-play an induction

32 **Communication strategies.** Kai is a German student on an internship in Scotland. He's talking to Brodie. Complete the dialogue with the phrases from the box.

I'm sorry, what are you making ■ it's a kind of ■ It's a thing you use ■ more like ■ What do you call that thing ■ What you are saying is that ■ you mean

1 Kai: I'm going to make Apfelstrudel.
Brodie: ______________________________?
Kai: Apfelstrudel, ______________________________ apple pie, but ______________ a roll. Do you have a …? Oh, how do I say this?
Brodie: What is it? What do you need?
Kai: ______________________________ to make the pastry flat.
Brodie: Yes, I know, ______________________________ a rolling pin!

2 Kai: ______________________________ you're wearing in the picture, the skirt?
Brodie: That's not a skirt, it's a kilt. Women wear skirts. Men wear kilts.
Kai: ______________________________ the same garment has a different name if it's worn by a man or by a woman?

33 **Your city.** Choose roles and do this role-play. You can video record it and show it to your class. You can do a real tour or use a map. Use phrases from the box.

Student A
Show Student B, an English exchange student, who speaks no German, some places in your city. You don't know the English names, so describe the places below verbally or non-verbally and add your own.
Rathaus, Bahnhof, Bushaltestelle, Jugendzentrum.

Student B
You are an English exchange student learning German and you want to find out the names of different places – more than just the ones Student A describes. You can show or demonstrate to Student A or you can paraphrase.

Paraphrasing: statements
It's a thing for … -ing. / It's a thing that you use to … / It's sort / kind of like a …
Paraphrasing: questions
What do you call the thing that you use to …? / What's it called when you …?
Asking for repetition
Sorry, what was that? / I'm sorry, what did you say?
Asking for clarification
Does that mean that …? / Have I got it right that …?
Rephrasing
What I mean is … / To put it another way, … / What you're saying is …

Mediation

34 Extraordinary jobs

a You want to create a wall newspaper about extraordinary jobs in your English class. For your project, each student presents one unusual job. You've found the following article about the job of a golf ball diver. Write an article of about 150 words about how a golf ball diver earns money, the equipment needed and disadvantages of this job.

Bis zu 1900 Prozent Rendite – das Geschäft mit dem „weißen Gold“ vom Golfplatz

Sascha Kruse taucht seit 17 Jahren in Norddeutschland professionell nach Golfbällen. Mehrere Tausend am Tag fischt er aus dem Wasser. Dahinter steckt ein bemerkenswertes Geschäftsmodell – für das er sogar seinen sicheren Job im Büro kündigte.

An einem typischen Tauchtag stehe ich um vier Uhr auf, steige ins Auto und fahre möglichst nah an die Einstiegsstelle am Golfplatz heran. An meinem Neoprenanzug sind 15 Kilo Blei befestigt, und die Sauerstoffflasche wiegt rund 20 Kilo. Später kommen mit Hunderten Golfbällen gefüllte Netze dazu. Da ist es praktisch, wenn der Wagen in der Nähe parkt.

Ich will möglichst immer um 5.30 Uhr im Wasser sein. Zumindest die flachen Stellen, wo mein Kopf aus dem Wasser ragt, muss ich vor den ersten Abschlägen abgehakt haben. Danach stelle ich ein Schild auf: Achtung Golfballtaucher! Dennoch sind mir schon mal Bälle um die Ohren gezischt.

Üblicherweise tauche ich an zwei bis drei Tagen in der Woche. Im stets trüben Wasser erschweren mir Algen, Schlingpflanzen, Wasserpest und Bisamratten die Suche. Zudem lauern Überraschungen: Einmal hat mir etwa ein Karpfen frontal eine verpasst.

Das Geschäftsmodell ist eine Win-win-Situation: Der Golfklub erlaubt mir das Abfischen des „weißen Goldes“, hat kunststofffreie Wasser und bekommt von mir eine Ablöse – acht bis zehn Cent pro Ball.

Dafür gehören die „Lake Balls“ danach mir, und ich kann sie auf meiner Website verkaufen. Ein Ball bringt je nach Güte zehn Cent bis 1,60 Euro – bei im Schnitt 2000 Bällen pro Tauchtag. Allerdings muss ich zu Hause noch tagelang waschen und sortieren.

Vertickt habe ich Golfbälle schon früh. Das kam so: Mit 14 düste ich mit dem Fahrrad nach dem Fußball an einem Golfplatz vorbei, plötzlich lag da ein Ball. Mit Kumpels stromerte ich durch die Hecken und las meine ersten Bälle auf.

Ich merkte: Die Golfer zahlen mir ein schönes Taschengeld. Irgendwann, schon nach der Lehre im Sportgeschäft, dachte ich mir: Im Wasser verlieren die Spieler doch noch mehr Bälle und da können sie vor allem nicht suchen.

So stieg ich 2003 größer ein. Erst nebenberuflich, vier Jahre später habe ich meinen Bürojob im Vertrieb einer Sporthandelsfirma gekündigt und habe im Alter von 28 ein Gewerbe als Golfballtaucher angemeldet. [...]

Mein Revier hat sich vergrößert: Ich betauche in Holstein, Hamburg und dem nördlichen Niedersachsen 35 Anlagen. Manche besuche ich alle zwei Jahre, andere vier- bis fünfmal pro Jahr. Das hängt von den Hindernissen ab: Je fieser, desto fetter die Beute.

Manchmal bekomme ich auch einen Spezialauftrag: Dann muss ich Handys, Golfschläger, Autoschlüssel, Brillen, Fahnenstangen und Hinweisschilder bergen.

Ein professioneller Golfballtaucher wird in Deutschland nicht reich, anders als die Kollegen in Florida. Allerdings können meine Frau, meine zwei Töchter und ich gut leben, [...]

Taken from: www. welt.de

b Here are some of the other extraordinary jobs that are presented on your wall newspaper. Tell your parents which of these jobs you would like to do and which job you wouldn't like to do. Give reasons. You can take notes in your exercise book.

[...] Gumologist
A Gumologist will spend their time tasting and bubble-testing gums before giving a final verdict and advising on new flavours. [...]

Dog Surfing Instructor
Passionate about pooches and partial to catching some waves? Then this job is definitely for you; put simply, you teach other people's dogs how to surf [...]

LEGO Builder
Ever been to LEGOLAND? All of those huge, amazing sculptures are impressive right? Well, someone's got to build them and that someone could be you! [...]

Waterslide Tester
For a pretty fair wage – £20,000 – the waterslide tester travels around the world, judging water slides on two things: "biggest splash" and "adrenaline factor". [...]

Taken from: www.coburgbanks.co.uk

My review

1 About making plans

a

1 degree
2 university
3 gap year
4 volunteer
5 abroad
6 internship
7 work experience

b

1 will be relaxing
2 will need
3 will have installed
4 Is he staying/Is he going to stay
5 is coming back/is going to come back
6 is studying/is going to study
7 are you thinking

2 About applications

1 Application
2 apply
3 advertised
4 passionate
5 volunteer
6 Ideally
7 Basically
8 Additionally
9 Naturally
10 considering
11 hearing
12 regards

3 About then and now

1 … I used to work for a local newspaper.
2 … so I didn't use to find it easy to concentrate.
3 … weekends used to be free.
4 the boss used to give me all the boring local assignments …
5 … I didn't use to get a proper break.
6 … I didn't use to worry about money …
7 Small newspapers like the one I used to work for …
8 … who used to buy a newspaper …

4 About volunteering and social issues

a

1 Advised … I decided …
2 Never having lived …, my experience …
3 Before applying
4 after arriving
5 working
6 Spending … meant …
7 While travelling
8 If asked

b

1 poverty/hunger
2 hunger/poverty
3 the homeless
4 the unemployed
5 single-parent
6 the young
7 debts
8 the elderly

We are family

1 Diverse family models

22 **a** Jackson and Oliver meet Emma in the school cafeteria. Listen to their conversation and complete the sentences.

1 A typical Australian is ______________________________ surf champion.

2 Oliver's dad comes from a family of ______________________________.
His mother's family background is ____________________. His grandmother is ________________ and his grandfather's ancestors are ______________________.

3 Jackson's parents are ______________________, but his mother's family is from ______________________. His father's family ___________________________ from Alberta and part of the family is ______________________________.

4 Cree is the aboriginal language with ______________________________ in Canada.

5 Emma and her family are all ______________________________. She looks like ____, with fair hair and blue eyes.

22 **b** Listen again and do the tasks below.

1 Summarize what they are talking about.

____

____

____

2 Explain why Emma doesn't think Oliver looks very Australian and what this comment reflects.

____

____

____

3 List the languages Oliver and Jackson speak.

____

____

4 Summarize what Jackson thinks about having a diverse family. Do you agree with him?

____

____

____

____

2 **The changing face of Canadian families.** Read about some changes in Canadian society. Complete the text with *be/get used to* and the correct form of the verb in brackets.

Over approximately the last fifty years, changes in Canadian society have led to new and diverse family structures. Canadians ______________________________ (1) (*have*) a traditional family structure consisting of a father, who had a job, married to a woman, who looked after their children full-time. As the years went by, things changed and Canadians ______________________________ (2) (*see*) women leaving traditional roles and going out to work. Other attitudes have changed, too. Although some people ______________________________ (3) (*not feel*) that foster and adoptive families were as valuable as other family structures, this is no longer the case. Nowadays, Canadian society ______________________________ (4) (*view*) families with gay, lesbian and bisexual couples the same way as any other family. In addition, with the increasing diversity of the country's population, a growing number of Canadian families ______________________________ (5) (*now have*) three generations living under one roof, a trend linked to contemporary immigration patterns.

3 **German family models**

a Choose the correct options to complete this article. Sometimes both are possible.

Social changes, **that/which** (1) include an increasing number of couples **that/who** (2) don't marry, influence the make-up of our society. **Even though/Although** (3) many family types **which are known/known** (4) today existed in the past, people's motives for selecting a specific family form have changed. The majority of families in Germany still represent the traditional model **which consists of/consisting of** (5) a father, mother and their child or children. **However/Therefore** (6), recent changes have led to an increase in other models: single parent families, step, adoptive, foster as well as same-sex families. In 2017, when a law was introduced **that/who** (7) gave same-sex couples the right to marry, a survey **conducted/conducting** (8) in Germany showed that about 70% of families were still traditional. **In addition/Furthermore** (9), the report revealed that many of these families were made up of unmarried couples **lived/living** (10) together. There are also 1.6 million single parents, **which/who** (11) are mostly women. Since 1995, the percentage of same-sex couples, **that/which** (12) can be two men or women, with children has more or less doubled, **whilst/but** (13) the number of families with several generations **who live/living** (14) under one roof has decreased considerably.

>>> **b** Describe these family models in your own words. Write in your exercise book.

1 step family **2** adoptive family **3** foster family

Practice: The new normal

4 READING FOCUS: Blue for a boy ...

a Read this article and complete it with the letters A – E for the missing sections.

What images come to mind when you think of the colour pink? Do you think of pink as a neutral colour? Many people think of pink as a colour for girls. ______ (1)

Many centuries ago, this colour coding just didn't exist. During the Renaissance, colours identified caste and class, not gender. Dyes were difficult to produce, and pink, which was particularly expensive, was used by the male elite. ______ (2)

______ (3) Then, softer colours or pastels became fashionable. Baby boys and girls were dressed in a wide range of pastels, and pink was even considered to be a masculine colour. In old books, pink was popular for boys because it is related to red. Red was seen as passionate, active and aggressive, which were thought to be typical masculine qualities.

______ (4) However, this trend started to decline in the 1970s. People thought that dressing young girls in feminine clothing would limit their opportunities for success, and many parents began choosing neutral colours. Nowadays, more men wear pink thanks to fashion brands that have made the colour popular and also because of a change in attitude. ______ (5)

A Also, in general, the younger generations don't have the prejudices their fathers and grandfathers had about pink being a colour for girls.

B Before the 20th century, boys and girls mostly wore white dresses until they were about six, which was very practical as white cotton could be easily bleached.

C If you see newborn babies in a hospital in many countries, you'll probably see them in pink or blue outfits to identify them as boys or girls. But it was not always like this.

D It wasn't until after WWII when established choices changed. In the 1940s, pink became the colour for girls and blue for boys.

E On the other hand, blue, which was made from ground lapis lazuli, an expensive semi-precious mineral, was often used to depict the Virgin Mary, who is the woman who most represented honour and virtue for Christians.

b Find words in the text that mean the same as:

1 a group with the same social or professional status: ______________________

2 a socially constructed identity: ______________________

3 a substance used to add colour to cloth: ______________________

4 to represent something in a picture or story: ______________________

5 make something lose its colour: ______________________

5 Like a girl

a You are going to watch a video about stereotypes. Before you watch, discuss what 'like a girl' could mean when talking about certain actions, like running.

5 **b** Watch the video and describe the difference between how the older girls and boys do the actions, and how the younger girls do them.

5 **c** Watch the video again, then choose one of the quotes and explain who is talking and what he or she is talking about. Make notes.

1 It sounds like you're trying to humiliate someone.
2 I think it definitely drops their self-confidence and really puts them down, because during that time they're already trying to figure themselves out.
3 If you're still scoring, and you're still getting to the ball on time, and you're still being first, you're doing it right. It doesn't matter what they say.

____

____

____

____

____

____

6 Comparing Canada and Estonia.

23 Listen to this class conversation about family life in Canada and Estonia and decide which country the quotes refer to.

		Estonia	Canada
1	... couples still divide most household chores along traditional lines ...		
2	... she always worked, and the mothers of my friends, too.		
3	Women usually earn less than men ...		
4	Sometimes they even make more money than men and they're the breadwinners.		
5	There are people, mostly men, who still think that it is better for the family if the husband is the main breadwinner ...		
6	... mothers can go to work when the child is six months old, ...		

7 Life in Canada.

The information below summarizes what Jackson says. Rewrite it in your exercise book using relative clauses and adding commas where necessary.

1 Quite a few women do jobs like childcare or looking after the elderly. These jobs are part-time and badly paid.
2 There is a majority of men and women. They will say that household work should be shared equally when both parents work.
3 Jackson's parents work full-time. They have always shared chores.

8 **Gender stereotypes.** Read this article about gender stereotypes. Put the missing phrases (A – G) back in the correct place. Use non-defining relative clauses and add the correct relative pronouns.

A are often reluctant to take advice anyway
B carried out a survey of 13- to 21-year olds
C makes prevention difficult
D revealed that young people characterize violence as encompassing a range of behaviours
E was often seen as an understandable response for a girl
F were interviewed face-to-face and online
G were widely regarded as being more emotional and fragile than men

Teenagers' opinions about when violence is acceptable or not can be influenced by the way they perceive relationships between men and women. The Zero Tolerance Charitable Trust, ______________________________ (1), found that nearly half of young people surveyed thought that it was acceptable for a man to act aggressively towards his female partner. In addition, three quarters of young men and more than half of young women surveyed thought the woman was 'often' or 'sometimes' to blame for such violence.

In a recent survey with 14 and 15-year-olds in the north of England, ______________________________ (2), young people, ______________________________ (3), said that they do not see all violence as 'bad'. Some violence is even seen as acceptable or deserved. Violence by women towards men, ______________________________ (4), was not viewed as significant. Girls, ______________________________ (5), were viewed as physically weaker and their potential to hurt or cause harm when they used violence was negligible.

Just telling young people, ______________________________ (6), that violence is wrong will not prevent them from accepting it. Young people's understanding of violence is largely influenced by their views on gender, ______________________________ (7).

Taking into account that gender appears to be a primary influence on their views on violence, schools should prioritize teaching about equality between the genders, stereotypes, sexism, sexual and gender pressures and gender-based harassment.

True friends

9 Peer pressure: good or bad?

24 **a** Some parents and teenagers share their views on peer pressure. Listen to the first part of the interview and summarize what Nina, David, Zoey and Oscar say in your exercise book.

25 **b** Listen to the second part. Are these statements true or false? Correct the false statements in your exercise book.

		True	False
1	David gets upset if friends don't invite him to their homes.	☐	☐
2	He is experiencing a lot of peer pressure right now.	☐	☐
3	He won't do something he likes unless his friends do it, too.	☐	☐
4	His mother expects the situation to change in the future.	☐	☐
5	Nina's friends thought she wasn't cool enough because she didn't have the same things they had.	☐	☐
6	She had to reflect on what her friends are really like.	☐	☐

10 Stress it!

Rewrite these sentences from the interview with emphatic pronouns or *do*.

1 I don't feel any kind of peer pressure, but some people want to be cool so badly that they will go to great lengths to do whatever.

____

______________________________.

2 I don't care what other people do or say.

______________________________.

3 Peer pressure leads you away from the person you really are.

______________________________.

4 If David knows two of his friends are going to another friend's place, and he's not going, he notices, and he gets quite upset.

____

______________________________.

5 I don't think he has a lot of influence from peers at the moment. He's still enthusiastic to try everything.

____

______________________________.

6 She did some real soul searching in terms of what friendship means.

______________________________.

11 **Peer influence.** Complete this article with the words and phrases from the box.

close to ■ compare to ■ fit in ■ grow up ■ identify with ■ involved in ■ rely on ■ similar to

Peers play an important role in the social and emotional development of children. It is natural, healthy and important for children to have and ____________________ (1) friends as they ____________________ (2). Your peers are people of your age or ________________ (3) it with experiences and interests ____________________ (4) yours. As you become more independent, your peers play a greater role in your life and they may feel like an extended family. These peers also influence you by the way they dress and act, things they are ________________________ (5), and the attitudes they show. It's totally natural for people to ________________________ (6) and ____________________ themselves __________ (7) their peers. Teenagers especially, are influenced by peers because they want to ____________________ (8).

12 **Pressure to conform.** Use the letters A – F to complete the second part of the article.

A into doing something you are uncomfortable with
B it is not always easy to resist negative peer pressure
C look to others for clues about what is and isn't acceptable
D peers can have a profoundly positive influence on each other
E to do something so they are accepted
F your friends will be quick to tell you when they think you're making a mistake

Peers may pressure you _____ (1), such as shoplifting or taking dangerous risks. The pressure to conform can be hard to resist. A young person might feel pressure _____ (2). When people are unsure of what to do in a social situation, they naturally _____ (3). However, _____ (4). Among peers you can find friendship and acceptance and share experiences that can build lasting bonds. Peers can help you make decisions and give you good advice. _____ (5), and many young people listen to their friends more than their parents. Your peer group gives you opportunities to try out new social skills, build relationships and work out differences. _____ (6), but when you do, you will feel good about it. It often takes one person to speak out to change a situation.

Practice: Is it love?

13 Teen well-being

a Read and discuss this article from a teenager website. Find a heading for each section.

The importance of mindfulness

____

From peer pressure to friendship drama and even violence at school, the stress levels of teenagers are rising. ______(1), for example: depression, anxiety, family problems and illness. Many of them are also dealing with difficult circumstances in their communities related to trauma, poverty, violence, racism and, more recently, the pandemic. It is not surprising that improving mental health is a major concern for parents and educators.

____

Mindfulness is an ancient practice that's been brought into modern medicine by Dr Jon Kabat-Zinn of the University of Massachusetts. Mindfulness means paying full attention to something on purpose and without thinking about anything else. ______(2)

____

Mindfulness can be used when teens need to focus their attention on something specific and not allow distractions to derail them. ______(3).

____

Mindfulness can also give teens a tool to cope with frustration when they are faced with something difficult. ______(4), allowing them to take a break, come back to the present moment, and re-discover their inner strengths.

____

Mindfulness is about getting teens to reflect on their own thoughts and actions and learn how to make better choices. ______(5). When teens understand, they not only make better choices but also feel more in control of their decision-making processes.

b Complete the sentences with the best words. Then complete the gaps 1–5 in **a** with sentences A–E.

A Research shows that **escaping/practising/avoiding** mindfulness can improve attention spans – including young people with ADHD who often have trouble concentrating.
B They are no longer reacting to things in their environment, but responding to them in thoughtful and **purposeful/random/obvious** ways.
C It means **sitting still/slowing down/speeding up** and really taking notice of what you are doing, even if it means just focusing on your breathing.
D Medical specialists say that teenagers are **dealing with/ignoring/depending on** complex health issues and many of them are stress-related.
E It helps them to stop automatic reactions, which are often **beneficial/horrible/harmful** to themselves and others.

14 Caring, complimenting, criticizing

26 **a** Listen to three conversations. Which one is caring, which complimenting and which criticizing? Describe what is happening. Speculate who is talking to who and what sort of relationships the conversations reveal.

Conversation 1 ____________________

____

Conversation 2 ____________________

____

Conversation 3 ____________________

____

27 **b** Listen to a family counsellor talking about teenage relationships. Tick (✓) the topics she speaks about and number them in the correct order.

- ☐ Equality ______
- ☐ Good communication ______
- ☐ Honesty ______
- ☐ Mutual respect ______
- ☐ Separate identities ______
- ☐ Support ______
- ☐ Trust ______

»» **c** Summarize what the counsellor says about each of the items that you ticked in **b**.

____

____

____

____

____

____

____

d Make the sentences more emphatic with emphatic pronouns or a form of the verb *do*.

1 I was in such a situation when I was a teenager so I speak from experience.

____________________.

2 You need to step back from the dizzying sensation of being swept off your feet and think.

____________________.

3 You need to have give-and-take in your relationship.

____________________.

4 And you should also feel free to keep developing new talents or interests.

____________________.

15 **WRITING FOCUS: I need advice.** Read these letters to an advice column in a teen magazine and write a reply to Irene or to Ben (120 – 150 words).

What is going to happen? My friend stole something from a shop and I was with her! I went to a shop with my best friend and she tried a hat on, then we got in the car and I drove her home. I looked over at her and she had the same hat on! I asked her if she had bought it because I didn't remember seeing her pay for it. She said she had walked out with it. I was shocked, but she didn't look worried about it at all. Now I'm freaking out. I thought about going back to the shop to say my friend didn't realize she had it on her head. And I'd offer to pay for it. But then I thought I'd be admitting I was involved in the theft and they would arrest me. I'm not sure what to do. Can you help me?
Irene

I have been with my current partner for about six months and I thought she was the girl of my dreams. But I suddenly realized that I have no friends anymore.
My girlfriend is obsessively jealous and suspects that I'm having an affair with one of my classmates but I'm not. This girl and I have been friends since kindergarten and she's like a sister to me, besides she's my brother's girlfriend! She's always saying I look at other girls and if she sees me talking to anyone, she starts making a scene. And if she calls me and she sees I'm online, she texts me over and over about who I was online with.
If I say I'm going to leave her, she threatens to hurt herself and what was once fun now feels suffocating and scary. I have allowed her to separate me from all those who could have helped me, including friends who warned me at the beginning, but I ignored them because I thought they were jealous. What can I do?
Ben

Describing a diagram (1)

16 **Understanding the information.** Look at this information about the effects of inclusive education. Explain what the diagrams show using the language in the TIP box.

A

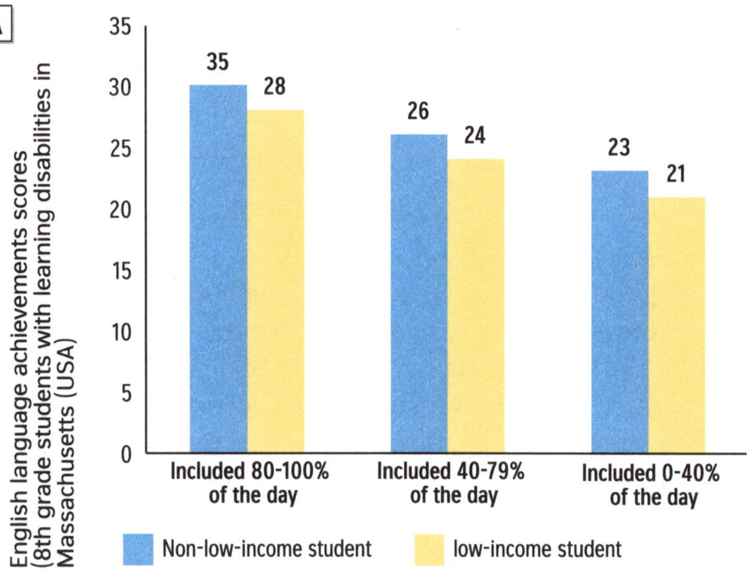

B

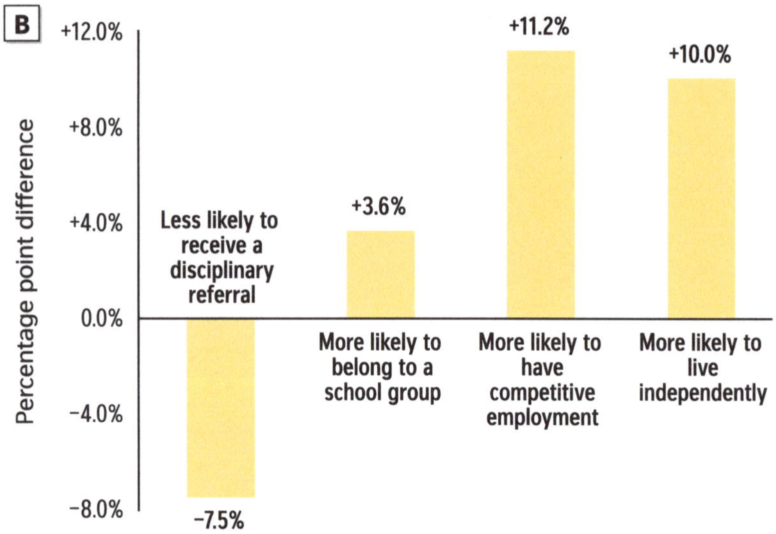

Background:
The most recent comprehensive review of the benefits of inclusive education was undertaken by the Alana Institute and presented in an international report entitled 'A Summary of the Evidence on Inclusive Education'.
It documents the results of 280 studies from 25 countries.

TIP

Useful language for describing data

Describing the diagram
The graph / bar chart shows … / gives information about / figures for … / compares …

Describing / Explaining change
By (*date*), the figure had fallen / declined / risen / increased to / levelled off / reached a peak …
There has been a (dramatic / rapid) rise / increase / fall / decline in (the number / percentage of) …

Comparing data
The majority / A small minority of people think / believe that …
Less / More than / Under (00)% / a half think / believe that …
A smaller / larger percentage (of) … / 6 out of 10 … Smaller numbers of / Fewer … compared with …. /
In contrast, …

Concluding
Overall, … / In conclusion, … /
In summary, …

17 **Write a description. Organize your text into paragraphs and write your description.**

- Introduction: Outline what information the diagrams give and what the survey is based on.
- Paragraph 2: Describe the highest statistics.
- Paragraph 3: Describe the lower statistics and those that show no change.
- Conclusion: Say what can be seen from the survey.

Youth crime and the law

18 **Different crimes.** Match the type of crime with the correct description.

1	blackmail	a	attacking and robbing someone in a public place
2	burglary	b	getting money by cheating people
3	fraud	c	intentionally killing a person
4	hijacking	d	stealing from someone or somewhere
5	mugging	e	breaking into someone's home
6	murder	f	demanding money from someone by threatening to expose secrets about them
7	robbery	g	using threats or violence to take control of a plane, vehicle or ship

19 **Youth crime in Canada**

a Complete the article with the correct words and phrases from the box.

> according to ■ also ■ at least ■ rather than ■ whenever possible ■ which ■ while ■ who

Criminal activity by Canadian youth has significantly declined both year-over-year and over the past decade. ______________________ (1) the latest Statistics Canada examination of police-reported crime, between 2010 and 2020, the rate of youth accused of crime fell by 63%.

______________________ (2) the report suggests that the impacts of the Covid-19 pandemic ______________________ (3) partly influenced the large decline in youth crime across Canada, it ______________________ (4) acknowledged the Youth Criminal Justice Act for its apparent role in longer-term reductions in youth crime rates. The Youth Criminal Justice Act is the law that governs Canada's youth justice system and it applies to minors ______________________ (5) are between the ages of twelve and eighteen years old, who are alleged to have committed criminal offences. The aim of the Act is to divert young people away from the criminal justice system ______________________ (6) as well as to focus on rehabilitation ______________________ (7) on punishment. The Act introduced changes to address concerns about the youth justice system ______________________ (8) included the overuse of the courts in less serious cases, unfairness of sentences, a lack of effective reintegration of young people released from custody, and the need to better take into account the interests of victims.

b Decide if these sentences are true, false or not in the text (NT). Correct the false sentences.

		True	False	NT
1	In the ten-year period reviewed, the number of minors accused of committing crimes dropped considerably.	☐	☐	☐
2	It seems that the Youth Criminal Justice Act has a positive impact on the reduction of offences.	☐	☐	☐
3	The Act aims to increase the severity of sentences.	☐	☐	☐
4	Before the introduction of the Act, minors and adults who committed crimes were given the same sentences.	☐	☐	☐
5	Before the Act, Canada had a very efficient reintegration programme.	☐	☐	☐

____

____

____

20 **Crime scene.** Read the statements and write sentences using *if*-sentences type 2 or 3.

1 The suspect left his wallet at the crime scene and that's why the police caught him.

______________________________.

2 The accused is not under 18 which is why she has to go to jail.

______________________________.

3 He stole something small from a supermarket, which is why he had to pay a fine.

______________________________.

4 The crime rate dropped because the Youth Criminal Justice Act was introduced.

______________________________.

5 The man spent eight months in jail last year because he stole a car.

______________________________.

21 **If only!** Complete the sentences with some of the verbs from the box.

> didn't have ■ wouldn't have ■ hadn't stolen ■ wouldn't have stolen ■ remembered ■ would remember ■ wouldn't be ■ wouldn't have been

1 If Ben hadn't been so stupid, he ______________ in court now.

2 If Tim ______________ cigarettes from the local supermarket, he wouldn't have to do community service every weekend for six months.

3 I'm sure my best friend ______________ so many problems now if her parents had helped her more when she was younger.

4 If only my old neighbour ______________ to lock her door every night, burglars wouldn't have been able to get into her house so easily last week.

Practice: Healthy living?

22 You are what you eat …

a Kevin gave a presentation about eating healthily. Complete one of his slides with suitable words from the box. There are two you don't need.

avoid ■ consume ■ contribute ■ encourage ■ prevent ■ reduce ■ rescue ■ save

You are what you eat, so ____________________ (1) less meat!

This will help:

- ____________________ (2) greenhouse gases
- ____________________ (3) the Amazon rainforest
- farm animals ____________________ (4) pain and suffering
- ____________________ (5) towards reducing antibiotic resistance
- ____________________ (6) diseases

b Kevin asked his classmates to complete this mini questionnaire. First answer the questions alone, then compare your answers in class.

1 How often do you eat meat as part of a meal?

☐ **A** never ☐ **C** two or three times a week

☐ **B** once a week ☐ **D** every day

2 Why do / don't you eat meat?

____

____

3 How could you change your eating habits to develop a healthier lifestyle?

____

____

23 Amelia's talk. Listen to another talk, then do the tasks in your exercise book.

28

1 Summarize the pros and cons of Kevin's position.

2 Explain the difference between a vegetarian and a vegan diet.

3 List the advantages and disadvantages of a vegan diet that Amelia mentions in her talk.

→ students' book, pages 102/103

24 Amelia's blog

a After her talk about the pros and cons of a vegan diet, Amelia posted a podcast. Check the meaning of these words and expressions from the podcast. Use a dictionary and write the definitions in your exercise book.

1 ethical	2 fake	3 soy	4 fibre	5 nutrients
6 processed	7 sodium	8 blood pressure	9 allergen	10 celiac

29 **b** Listen and answer the questions in your exercise book.

1 Why do more and more people eat plant-based food?
2 What is the calorific difference between real meat and plant-based meat?
3 Why could fake meats be a problem for people with high blood pressure?

25 Feedback. Amelia, Kevin and some friends talk about the lesson. Complete what they say with the correct form of the verbs to make type 2 or 3 *if*-sentences or mixed conditionals.

1 It's absolutely clear that if we ____________ (*do*) without industrial farming, we ____________ (*reduce*) greenhouse gas emissions.
2 But is that really a good idea? If we ____________ (*stop*) all meat consumption, it ____________ (*probably mean*) financial ruin for small meat farmers. It ____________ (*be*) much better if we ____________ (*cut down*) on our meat consumption and ____________ (*eat*) more vegetable-based food.
3 Not all that food is good. If my mother ____________ (*not check*) the ingredients of the 'healthy' food I had asked her to get for my party last weekend, she ____________ (*not find out*) that it wasn't very healthy.
4 But most of us really do need to change our eating habits. Look at me for example! If I ____________ (*not change*) my diet, I'm absolutely sure I ____________ (*be*) very overweight now.
5 If young people ____________ (*not suffer*) so much pressure from the fashion industry, they ____________ (*not have*) eating disorders.

26 SPEAKING FOCUS: The importance of food

a What do you think about the facts Kevin and Amelia presented? How important is food in our lives? How important is body image for you? Discuss with a partner.

b Work together to plan a healthy brunch for a group of friends. Present your ideas to the class. Who has the tastiest and healthiest menu?

27 Body image

a Complete this article on body image with words and phrases from the box.

an impact on ■ average weight ■ distorted body image ■ objective perception ■ on the other hand ■ overweight ■ plus-size mannequin ■ promoted ■ standard sizes ■ subjective image ■ the gap ■ vast majority

Body images

Body image is the ______________________ (1) we have of our own body, which is distinct from how our body actually appears. The way we see ourselves and our bodies has ______________________ (2) our mental health and our relationships. A healthy body image involves having an ______________________ (3) of our appearance and the ability to differentiate our value as a person from the way we look. ______________________ (4), a negative body image, which often appears during childhood, is frequently characterized by being uncomfortable with our appearance, extreme dieting, eating disorders or constantly checking ourselves in the mirror.

In society, thinness is often ______________________ (5) as ideal. Slender children, especially girls, may be viewed as more athletic or attractive, while those who are ______________________ (6) or obese are ridiculed due to established stereotypes. This can begin as early as childhood.

The promotion of rake-thin models has created a ______________________ (7). For years, young girls and women have looked at thin models and seen themselves as overweight or even really fat in comparison. They try to imitate them and this has resulted in ______________________ (8) between the ideal body and real women being wider than ever. Stigmatizing women of ______________________ (9) on popular television shows sends negative signals, especially to adolescents.

The plus-size fashion movement started because the ______________________ (10) of people, often women, are larger than the ______________________ (11) demanded by the modelling industry. However, there are voices against it. A couple of years ago, a famous sports brand put a ______________________ (12) inside one of its stores dedicated to 'celebrating the diversity and inclusivity of sport'. It sparked outrage and debate on social media and the internet. A journalist wrote that obese mannequins are selling women a dangerous lie: that obesity is beautiful and healthy.

»» **b** Read the article again. Do you agree with it? Make notes in your exercise book. Then write a letter to the editor of the magazine giving your opinion (150–180 words).

Advertising and Generation Z

28 Gen Z shoppers

a Philip, a German student, has written a blog about the shopping habits of Generation Z. His spellchecker highlighted some mistakes. Choose the correct options to complete his post.

Hi folks

I hope you're all doing fine. Yesterday I raed (1) (**A** read / **B** red / **C** reads) an intresting (2) (**A** interest / **B** interested / **C** interesting) article about the shopping habits of Gen Z, which really made me think. As we all know, Gen Z is highly influential and spends more time than ever online, which disrupts traditional advertising strategies. The authors of the article explained that, when it comes to choice, Gen Zers trust their peers to help them find the best brands and products.

According to recent surveys, 44% of Generation Z have bought something reccomended (3) (**A** recommended / **B** recommend / **C** recommending) by a social influencer, and 70% of Gen Zers folows (4) (**A** following / **B** follow / **C** follows) at least one influencer. They also use a wide range of social media apps and about 40% have four or more social media accounts. The article argues that the popolaricy (5) (**A** popolarity / **B** popularity / **C** popularicy) of social media among Gen Z consuments (6) (**A** consumes / **B** consumers / **C** consents) has forced brands to work together with influencers. The authors claim our generation doesn't need a face-to-face relatonsship (7) (**A** relationsship / **B** relationships / **C** relationship) with someone to feel connected to them. But that is what modern technology makes us do. I totally agree with that! Older generations used to have role models. I don't need them. Do you? I want someone who is autentically (8) (**A** authenticc / **B** authentic / **C** authentically) and reliable. What I hate is when I have the fleeling (9) (**A** fleeing / **B** feeling / **C** flying) that an influencer is just trying to sell me something. What do you think? If you want to have your opponion (10) (**A** opinionn / **B** opposite / **C** opinion) heard, this is the place to do it! All comments welcome.

b Decide if the following sentences are true, false or not in the text (NT). Correct the false ones in your exercise book.

		True	False	NT
1	Gen Z has changed the way brands advertise their products.	☐	☐	☐
2	Gen Zers rely on online or printed ads to buy what is fashionable.	☐	☐	☐
3	The choice of products is largely determined by the recommendation of influencers.	☐	☐	☐
4	Gen Z still considers face-to-face interaction essential to establish meaningful communication.	☐	☐	☐
5	They expect influencers to only sell them a product.	☐	☐	☐
6	Philip buys most of his clothes online.	☐	☐	☐

29 Being an influencer

30 a Listen to an interview with Sophie, a Gen Z influencer. Tick (✓) the topics she speaks about.

☐ 1 her beginnings as an influencer
☐ 2 her holidays
☐ 3 ethical fashion
☐ 4 her relationship with her family
☐ 5 her work in the community
☐ 6 building a community of followers

30 b Listen again and tick (✓) the problems she mentions.

☐ 1 child labour
☐ 2 health and safety
☐ 3 use of dangerous substances
☐ 4 cruelty to animals
☐ 5 exploitation of workers
☐ 6 having a healthy diet

30 Being emphatic.

Make these sentences more emphatic using the words in brackets. Make any necessary changes without changing the meaning. Write the sentences in your exercise book.

1 GenZ is disrupting brand strategies across the globe. (*It …*)
2 This social group spends more time than ever online. This is the first time something like this has happened. (*Never before …*)
3 A Gen Zer does not need a face-to-face relationship with someone to feel connected to them. (*What …*)
4 I rarely meet young people who know what ethical fashion is. (*Rarely …*)
5 This whole niche of people who promote ethical fashion brands inspired me to start blogging. (*It …*)
6 I'm not saying that you have to be online 24/7, but make sure you reply. (*In no way …*)

31 Social media language.

31 Listen to the final part of the interview with Sophie. She uses some language that is common in social media. Listen and find words that mean the same as:

1 a prompt to get your audience to do something specific: ____________________
2 a symbol used to identify or search for subjects of interest: ____________________
3 when someone mentions you on their social media profile and asks their followers to check out your page: ____________________
4 a piece of writing that is published on the internet: ____________________
5 information that shows where something has been posted: ____________________
6 an announcement that someone likes your post: ____________________

→ students' book, pages 106/107

Practice: Digital communication

32 **Technology in the modern world.** Read the article about internet communication and find a good heading. Give reasons for your choice. Then, complete the article with the prepositions from the box. You will need some more than once.

by ■ for ■ from ■ in ■ of ■ on ■ over ■ to ■ towards ■ with

____

Technology is a huge part ________ (1) the modern world and impacts nearly all aspects of our lives – language included. However, the influence of technology ________ (2) language is not only positive and it has been the subject of some critical reports. One thing critics commented ________ (3) is the impossibility of showing emotions online, ________ (4) example sarcasm or sadness. Well those days are over. Welcome ________ (5) the world of memes! Memes are hard to miss in today's society – they are typical ________ (6) modern communication and you find them everywhere ________ (7) the internet. The term meme derives ________ (8) the Greek word *mimema,* meaning 'imitated' and it was introduced ________ (9) 1976 ________ (10) the British evolutionary scientist Richard Dawkins. He defined it as 'a unit of cultural transmission' in his work *The Selfish Gene*. Many years later, he referred ________ (11) an internet meme as one deliberately altered by human creativity. ________ (12) the early days of the meme, people would just look ________ (13) a popular picture and add text ________ (14) the top or bottom of it. These early memes did not really contribute much ________ (15) conveying emotions. The new age of memes began to give new shape to the way we communicate ________ (16) each other online. The internet meme has gained a new usage and has become an example ________ (17) a culture which is constantly recreated and shared ________ (18) people. The internet meme is collectively produced and can evolve and change ________ (19) time. A meme has no one specific author and there is no finished form, so who knows what we can look forward ________ (20) in the future!

33 **Impact of technology.** Make these sentences more emphatic using the words in brackets. Make any necessary changes without changing the meaning. Write in your exercise book.

1 Technology impacts nearly all aspects of our lives – language included. (*What* ...)
2 Technology also impacts language. (*What* ...)
3 One thing critics have observed is the impossibility of showing emotions online. (*What* ...)
4 Memes are hard to miss in today's society because they have taken over the internet. (*It* ...)
5 British evolutionary biologist Richard Dawkins introduced the word 'meme' in his work *The Selfish Gene* in 1976. (*It* ...)

34 **Cyberbullying.** Read this article and choose the correct linking words and phrases from the box to complete it. Sometimes more than one answer is correct.

additionally ■ although ■ as a result ■ consequently ■ however ■ in addition ■ in conclusion ■ in fact ■ therefore ■ while

The increase in internet communication and limitations imposed by the Covid-19 pandemic lockdowns have resulted in people engaging in fewer real interactions and more cyber relationships. ______________________ (1), experts claim that the use of technology does not provide the connectedness that real communication does. ______________________ (2), it often increases the feeling of being alone. ______________________ (3), many people are losing their ability to empathize and can often end up making thoughtless statements. ______________________ (4), experiences and emotions are often exaggerated for effect. ______________________ (5), there has been a dramatic increase in cyberbullying.

The most common type of harassment young people encounter online is name-calling. ______________________ (6), some teens say false rumours are spread about them on the internet, ______________________ (7) others have had someone constantly asking where they are, who they're with or what they're doing or have been the target of physical threats online.

Sometimes, people are afraid or not sure if they really are being bullied or not. ______________________ (8), they do nothing about it. If you think you're being bullied, or know someone who is, report any upsetting messages or posts immediately. Speak up until you find someone to help. Don't respond, and never forward the message. Ignoring bullies is the best way to take away their power, but it isn't always easy to do. ______________________ (9) you should not respond to a bully, it is a good idea to save evidence of the bullying. It can help you prove your case, if needed.

______________________ (10), nobody has to be alone or live in fear. Help is out there, but some people need help finding it.

35 **Gen Zers.** Make these sentences more formal and emphatic. Use the expressions in brackets.

1 GenZ are rarely seen without their mobile phones in their hands. (*Rarely …*)

____

____.

2 A brand will not win them over unless it approaches them with authenticity and engages them on the channels and platforms where they're most receptive. (*In no way …*)

____

____.

3 We seldom escape from the impact of technology on our lives. (*Hardly ever …*)

____

____.

4 You will almost never see Gen Zers influenced by traditional celebrities or publicity. (*Rarely …*)

____

____.

36 **LISTENING FOCUS: The influence of advertising**

32 **a** Listen to a radio programme where some teenagers discuss the influence of advertisements on young people. Who admits they are influenced by advertisements and who claims not to be?

32 **b** Listen again and decide who mentions the following.

1 Marianne	**a** The products aren't as good as the ads show.
2 Luke	**b** Advertisements can create eating and psychological problems.
3 Brianne	**c** Advertisements have changed.
4 Kath	**d** Society should change some of its values.
5 Leo	**e** Advertisements can influence someone in ways they are unaware of.
6 Megan	**f** Advertising makes us want to buy the products they show.

c Focus on one student and summarize what he or she thinks about advertising.

____

____

____

____

____

____

____

»» **d** Explain what you think about advertising. Think about how much it influences you and your peers. Ask a few of your classmates and record a short video explaining your opinions.

Describing diagrams (2)

37 **Write a description.** Look at the diagrams, then write a short description of the information and summarize the main findings. Use the expressions in the box and refer to the TIP box on page 68.

> by comparison ■ cut across ■ demographic groups ■ four-in-ten ■ more than twice as likely ■ one-in-five ■ on the rise ■ roughly equal shares ■ seven-in-ten ■ six-in-ten teens ■ three-in-ten ■ top the list

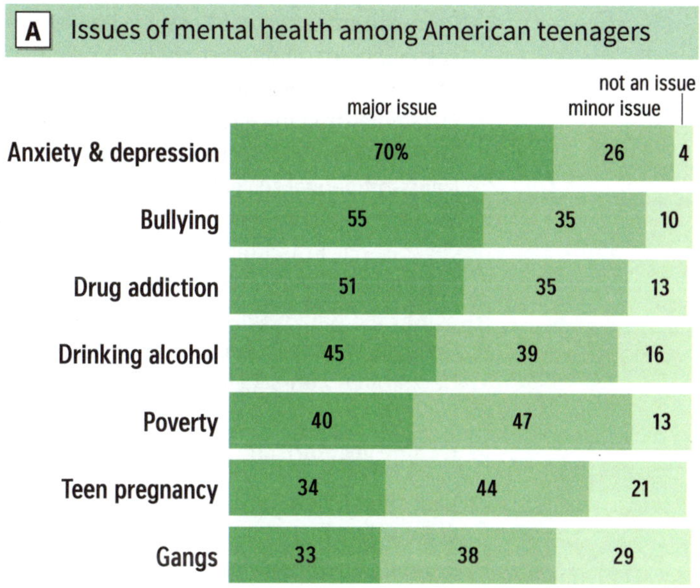

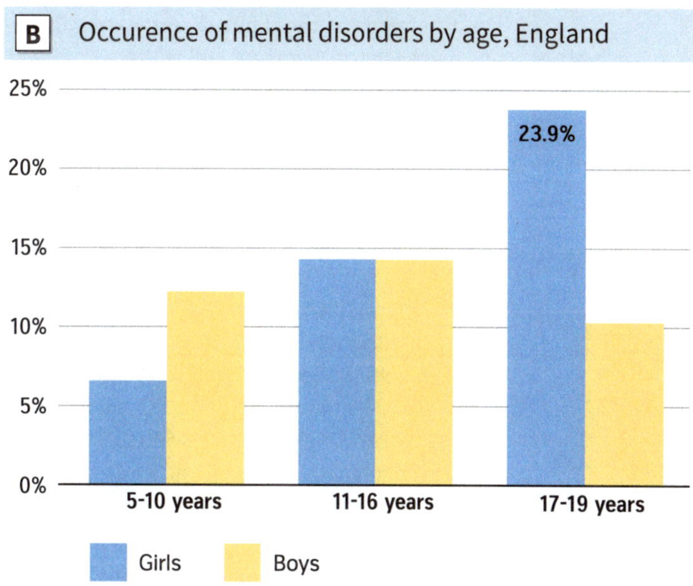

Sources: Pew Research Center (A), NHS (B)

38 **Do your research.** Look for information and diagrams on the same topic about young people in Germany. Copy or draw your own diagram, then make notes.

39 **Present your findings.** Compare the data with what you have already learned and present your findings to the class.

→ students' book, pages 110/111

Mediation

40 Vegetarian food

a You tell your English friend Oliver that you are considering becoming vegetarian. You read an article about vegetarian diets and use the information in it to answer Oliver's questions.

Wer sich vegetarisch ernährt, verzichtet auf Fleisch, Fisch und Nahrungsmittel, die tierische Produkte enthalten wie Gelatine. Das kann viele gesundheitliche Vorteile haben. Allerdings sollten Vegetarier sich intensiv mit der Zusammenstellung ihrer Nahrung auseinandersetzen, um einen potenziellen Nährstoffmangel zu vermeiden.
Es gibt zahlreiche Gründe, die für eine vegetarische Ernährung sprechen. Vielen Vegetariern liegt das Wohl der Tiere oder der Schutz des Klimas sehr am Herzen, andere verzichten für ihre Gesundheit auf Fisch, Fleisch und Geflügel. Welche Vorteile hat diese Ernährungsform tatsächlich? Ist ein Mangel an bestimmten Nährstoffen wahrscheinlich?

Ist eine vegetarische Ernährung gesund?

Laut einer Erhebung des Robert Koch-Instituts ernähren sich etwa 4,3 Prozent der Erwachsenen vegetarisch. [...]
Vegetarier nehmen viel Obst und Gemüse sowie Getreideprodukte zu sich. Das gilt als sehr gesund, was durch verschiedene Studien belegt ist. Unter anderem haben Vegetarier ein geringeres Risiko für Übergewicht und die Zuckerkrankheit Diabetes mellitus Typ 2. Auch Herz-Kreislauf-Probleme treten seltener auf. Sogar auf einige Krebsarten hat diese Ernährungsform vorbeugende Effekte, vor allem auf Darmkrebs. Mediziner betonen allerdings, dass die meisten Vegetarier zudem maßvoll mit Alkohol und Nikotin umgehen, sowie sich tendenziell häufiger bewegen. Vermutlich entstehen die deutlich messbaren Vorteile für die Gesundheit durch dieses Gesamtpaket.

Kann es durch eine vegetarische Ernährung zu Mangelerscheinungen kommen?

Die Deutsche Gesellschaft für Ernährung (DGE) empfiehlt, Fleisch und Wurst in Maßen zu sich zu nehmen – 300 bis 600 Gramm pro Woche, plus ein- bis zweimal pro Woche Fisch. Ein vollständiger Verzicht erhöht das Risiko für einen Mangel an jenen Vitaminen und Mineralstoffen, die normalerweise zu einem großen Teil über den Verzehr von Fleisch und Fisch aufgenommen werden. Das betrifft vor allem die Vitamine B12 und D sowie die Mineralstoffe Eisen, Kalzium, Zink, Jod und Selen. Auch ein Mangel an langkettigen n-3 Fettsäuren (Omega-3-Fettsäuren) kann entstehen. Gegebenenfalls kann darüber hinaus die Menge an Proteinen (Eiweiß) in der Nahrung zu gering sein. Grundsätzlich ist eine ausreichende Versorgung bei einer vegetarischen Ernährung aber durchaus möglich. Das heißt jedoch, dass Vegetarier darauf achten sollten, dass sie ihre Lebensmittel ausgewogen zusammenstellen.
Unter anderem können Getreideprodukte, Hülsenfrüchte und Nüsse dazu beitragen, einen Mangel an Nährstoffen zu vermeiden. Ein häufiger Verzehr von Hafer und Hirse beugt beispielsweise Eisenmangel vor. Empfohlen wird zudem, Hühnereier, Milch und Milchprodukte in ausreichenden Mengen in den Speiseplan einzubauen. Dann ist eine vegetarische Ernährung sogar für Personen mit erhöhtem Nährstoffbedarf möglich, etwa für Kinder und für Frauen während der Schwangerschaft.

Taken from: www.aok.de

Oliver You're thinking about going vegetarian. What exactly does vegetarianism mean?

You ____

____

____.

Oliver But if you don't eat these foods, won't you miss certain nutrients and vitamins?

You ____

____

____

____.

Oliver I can't imagine not eating any meat. Why do you think about doing without it?

You ____

____

____

____.

Oliver Are there many vegetarians in Germany?

You ____.

Oliver I don't think vegetarianism is for me. But if you really try it out, please tell me how you get on.

b Later Oliver emails you an infographic about meat consumption in the UK. You show it to your little sister and explain it to her. Note down the most important points here and use your exercise book to write a detailed description of the infographic.

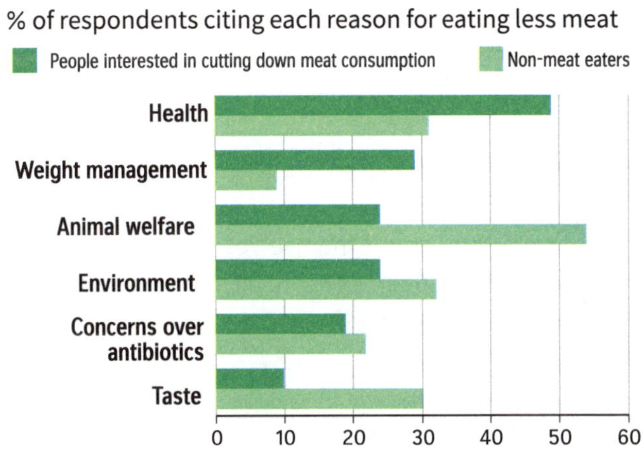

____

____

____

____

____

____

____

____

____

____

My review

1 About families

a

1 mixed union; 2 was used to being;
3 traditional; 4 divorced; 5 get used to living;
6 are used to packing; 7 get used to having;
8 same-sex; 9 blended; 10 extended

b

1 I love Vancouver, which was recently ranked the third most 'livable place in the world'.
2 My family, which consists of my mom and dad, my younger sister and my mom's new partner Cathy, is known as a blended family.
3 My mom, who came here with her parents when she was four, still has some family members in China.
4 My parents are mixed union – a term describing a couple of different national or ethnic origin.
5 Mom and Dad got divorced, forcing them to sell our family home.
6 We are a great example of family diversity in Canada, proving that the traditional nuclear family is no longer the only acceptable family form.

2 About making your point!

a

1 myself; 2 itself; 3 themselves; 4 herself;
5 ourselves; 6 himself; 7 itself; 8 themselves;
9 myself; 10 yourself

b

1 I did make a mistake.
2 She does understand how important it is.
3 You don't remember, but I did tell you.
4 Most parents do worry about their children.
5 They did know they were in trouble.
6 I do regret what happened.
7 Sam does feel he is often misunderstood.
8 You did promise to help me.

3 About crime and punishment

a

1 …, I wouldn't be in trouble now.
2 …, I would have a criminal record.
3 …, I wouldn't have got into trouble.
4 …, I wouldn't have committed the offence.
5 …, I would be in even more trouble than I am.
6 …, my mom would be devastated.
7 …, I wouldn't be in court now.
8 …, the judge would have sent me to jail last week.
9 What would you do if one of your friends dared you to steal something?
10 How would you react if one of your friends suggested doing something illegal?

b

1a If I hadn't wanted to impress my best friend, I wouldn't have stolen a T-shirt.
1b If I hadn't been caught, I wouldn't have to do thirty hours of community service now.
2a If Mary had taken the extra lessons, she might have passed her exams.
2b If Mary had passed her exams, she wouldn't have to retake the year.
3a If Tom had listened to his dad, he wouldn't have broken his neighbour's window.
3b If Tom hadn't broken his neighbour's window, he wouldn't have to pay £50.

4 About advertising tricks

1 It's the pop-up ads which …
2 What's unacceptable is …
3 It's this kind of sneaky advertising which …
4 What's really worrying is …
5 What's really annoying is …
6 Only later did I realize …
7 Never has an advertiser …
8 Rarely do you …
9 Not once did I …
10 In no way do I …

Appendix

Grammatical terms

Here are some of the most important **grammatical terms** in English:

active	aktiv
adjective	Adjektiv
adverb adverb of frequency adverb of manner adverb of place adverb of time	Adverb Adverb der Häufigkeit Adverb der Art und Weise Adverb des Ortes Adverb der Zeit
article definite article indefinite article	Artikel bestimmter Artikel unbestimmter Artikel
aspect	Aspekt
auxiliary	Hilfsverb
clause adverbial clause comment clause contact clause *if*-clause main clause relative clause defining relative clause non-defining relative clause subordinate clause (of time)	Teilsatz Adverbialsatz nicht notwendiger Relativsatz, der sich auf den gesamten Satz bezieht notwendiger Relativsatz ohne Relativpronomen Bedingungssatz; Konditionalis Hauptsatz Relativsatz notwendiger Relativsatz nicht notwendiger Relativsatz Temporalsatz
comparative	Komparativ; Vergleichsform
conditional conditional type I, II, III, mixed	Konditionalis; Konditionalsatz
demonstrative determiner	Demonstrativbegleiter
future future perfect future progressive future with *going to* future with *will* present progressive with future meaning simple present with future meaning	Futur; Zukunft Futur II Verlaufsform des Futur Futur mit *going to* Futur mit *will* Verlaufsform des Präsens mit Zukunftsbezug einfache Form des Präsens mit Zukunftsbezug
gerund	Gerundium
imperative	Imperativ; Befehlsform
infinitive *to*-infinitive	Infinitiv; Grundform *to*-Infinitiv
modal modal substitute	Modalverb Ersatzform eines Modalverbs
negative	negativ; verneinend
noun countable noun uncountable noun	Substantiv; Nomen zählbares Substantiv nicht zählbares Substantiv

object **direct object** **indirect object**	Objekt direktes Objekt indirektes Objekt
participle **participle construction** **past participle** **perfect participle** **present participle**	Partizip Partizipialkonstruktion Partizip Perfekt *having* + Partizip Perfekt Partizip Präsens
passive ***by*-agent**	Passiv Handelnde(r) im Passivsatz
past **simple past** **past progressive**	Präteritum; Vergangenheit einfache Form der Vergangenheit Verlaufsform der Vergangenheit
past perfect **past perfect** **past perfect progressive**	Plusquamperfekt einfache Form des Plusquamperfekts Verlaufsform des Plusquamperfekts
plural	Plural; Mehrzahl
positive	positiv; bejaht
possessive *'s*	*s*-Genitiv
possessive determiner	Possessivbegleiter
preposition **preposition of place** **preposition of time**	Präposition Präposition des Ortes Präposition der Zeit
present **simple present** **present progressive**	Präsens; Gegenwart einfache Form des Präsens Verlaufsform des Präsens
present perfect **present perfect** **present perfect progressive**	Perfekt einfache Form des Perfekt Verlaufsform des Perfekt
pronoun **indefinite pronoun** **interrogative pronoun** **object pronoun** **personal pronoun** **possessive pronoun** **reciprocal pronoun** **reflexive pronoun** **relative pronoun** **subject pronoun**	Pronomen Indefinitpronomen; unbestimmtes Pronomen Interrogativpronomen; Fragepronomen Objektpronomen Personalpronomen Possessivpronomen; besitzanzeigendes Pronomen Reziprokpronomen Reflexivpronomen Relativpronomen Subjektpronomen
prop word *one/ones*	Stützwort *one/ones*
quantifier	Numeral; Zahlwort
question **question tag**	Frage Frageanhängsel; Bestätigungsfrage
reported speech **backshift**	indirekte Rede Rücksetzung der Zeitform um eine Stufe
singular	Singular; Einzahl
statement	Aussagesatz
subject	Subjekt
superlative	Superlativ
tense	Zeitform
verb **irregular verb** **regular verb**	Verb; Tätigkeitswort unregelmäßiges Verb regelmäßiges Verb
word order	Wortstellung

Grammar

Do you have questions about grammar? The **grammar appendix** explains all the grammar that you learn in this book.

G 1 Present perfect and present perfect progressive (revision)

students' book, pages 14 – 15

We form the present perfect with *has / have* + past participle.

	has / have	past participle	
You boys	***have***	***had***	*such a good season so far.*
I	***'ve***	***been***	*to Australia twice.*
I	***haven't***	***been***	*to New Zealand.*
Jason	***has***	***known***	*Ricky since primary school.*
	Have *you*	***seen***	*Bruce recently?*

We form the present perfect progressive with *has / have been* + *-ing*.

	has / have been	*-ing*	
You boys	***have been***	***playing***	*so well.*
She	***has been***	***coaching***	*the rugby team for ten years.*
We	***haven't been***	***living***	*here for long.*
How long	***have*** *you* ***been***	***waiting****?*	

The present perfect connects the past and the present. This is usually an action or a situation in the past which is connected with or has a consequence in the present. It can also be something that started in the past and continues in the present.

- We use the present perfect to emphasize the result. We also use it to express 'how much / many'.
  Our partner school in Christchurch ***has invited*** *us to play in their rugby tournament.*
  *I****'ve tried*** *surfing many times, but I just can't do it.*
  *I****'ve been*** *to the outback several times.*

- We use the present perfect progressive to emphasize the duration of an action.
  The coach ***has been trying*** *to organize a trip like this for a while.*
  *I****'ve been working*** *in the café since April.*
  *We****'ve been training*** *hard all month.*

State verbs (e.g. *have, know, understand*) do not usually have a progressive form, so we use the present perfect when we are expressing the duration of an action.
*He****'s wanted*** *to take the team to play in New Zealand since he started coaching them.*
Eleni ***hasn't known*** *about Aunt Koula's illness for very long.*
NOT ~~*Eleni hasn't been knowing about Aunt Koula's illness for very long.*~~

Examples

*I****'ve tried*** *to fix the computer, but I can't find the problem.*
*I'm exhausted. We****'ve been driving*** *all day.*
How long ***have*** *you* ***been living*** *in Perth?*
How many and which Australian cities ***have*** *you* ***visited****?*
*We****'ve known*** *each other since kindergarten.*

G 2 Indefinite article after *such, quite, half*

students' book, pages 14 – 15

We use *such a / quite a / half a* + noun phrase. The noun phrase is often a noun on its own or an adjective + noun.
*She's **such a** great teacher.*
*It was **quite a** long journey.*
*I drank **half a** litre of water.*

Note that we use *such an / quite an / half an* before a vowel sound.
*It was **such an** amazing day.*
*It's **quite an** old idea.*
*It takes **half an** hour.*

G 3 Past perfect and past perfect progressive (revision)

students' book, pages 18 – 19

We form the past perfect with *had* + past participle.

	<u>*had*</u>	<u>past participle</u>	
I	***had***	***been***	*there twice already.*
She	***hadn't***	***seen***	*the film before.*
	***Had** they*	***met***	*before?*

We form the past perfect progressive with *had been* + *-ing*.

	<u>*had been*</u>	<u>*-ing*</u>	
We	***had been***	***driving***	*for about an hour.*
We	***hadn't been***	***living***	*there for long.*
How long	***had** you **been***	***waiting**?*	

- We use the past perfect (often with *already*) to show that one action or situation happened before another event or before a specific time in the past. We often connect the two events with time expressions such as *by the time, before, when, after* and *until*. We also use *by* + time / date.
  *Other European explorers **had** already **discovered** the new land by the time the British arrived.*
  *We went for a walk after we**'d eaten** lunch.*
  *We**'d finished** the meeting by mid-morning.*
- We use the past perfect progressive to focus on the length of the earlier action and to show that it was in progress before the second action started.
  *Aboriginal people **had been living** in Australia for thousands of years before the Europeans arrived.*
  *They**'d been waiting** for ages by the time we arrived.*

Examples
*I got to the station two minutes after the train **had left**.*
*I **had** never **been** to Sydney until last month.*
*We**'d been walking** for miles before we stopped for a rest.*

G 4 Passive – all tenses (revision)

students' book, pages 24 – 25

- We often use the passive when we do not mention who does the action. This is because we are more interested in what happens, or because the person who does the action is obvious, unknown or not important. The passive also means we can avoid using vague subjects like *someone, people* and *they*. The passive is often used in English when we use a construction with 'man' in German.
  The rugby world cup ***is held*** *every four years. It* ***was*** *first* ***held*** *in 1987.*
  Uluru ***has been designated*** *a UNESCO World Heritage Site.*

- However, we can use the passive with *by* to say who does the action. This is usually when we are giving new information about an existing topic. The passive enables us to put the existing information first and the new information second.
  New Zealand was first settled ***by the Maori people*** *as early as 1300 AD.*
  Busloads of tourists are brought here every day ***by big tour companies.***

We use the passive in different tenses. We form the passive with *be* + past participle.

- Simple present (*am / is / are* + past participle)
  Rugby union ***is played*** *by two teams of 15 players.*
  Many different crops ***are grown*** *in Australia.*

- Simple past (*was / were* + past participle)
  The president ***was elected*** *for a second term of office.*
  The Olympics ***were*** *first* ***held*** *in Australia in 1956.*

- Present progressive (*am / is / are being* + past participle)
  The room ***is being cleaned.***
  The election votes ***are being counted.***

- Past progressive (*was / were being* + past participle)
  My computer ***was being repaired.***
  The rooms ***were being cleaned.***

- Present perfect (*has / have been* + past participle)
  The election result ***has been announced.***
  Relations between Australia and New Zealand ***have*** *often* ***been compared*** *to those of cousins.*

- Past perfect (*had been* + past participle)
  The beach hut ***had been cleaned*** *when we got back.*

- We form a question by putting the subject after the auxiliary verb *be or* between the auxiliaries if there are two of them.
  When ***was*** *Parliament House* ***built****?*
  Has *the World Cup ever* ***been held*** *in Australia?*

Examples

Australia ***was*** *first* ***named*** *Terra Australis, which* ***was*** *later* ***abbreviated*** *to the current form.*
When ***was*** *Australia first* ***settled*** *by Europeans?*
Is *Australia Day* ***celebrated*** *on the same date each year?*
It ***is believed*** *that Australia* ***has been inhabited*** *for at least 40,000 years.*

G 5 Passive with verb + preposition

students' book, pages 24 – 25

When a verb is followed by a preposition, the preposition stays in the same position in the passive.
Each nation has its own Creation legends which ***have been passed down*** *by the Elders.*
We can make sure the place ***is looked after.***
At the hotel, all diets ***are catered for.***

Examples

Their hotel room ***was broken into.***
The meeting ***has been called off.***
Today, most goods ***are paid for*** *electronically.*

G 6 Passive: verbs with two objects

students' book, pages 24 – 25

Some active verbs have two objects. There are two possible structures. Note that the **direct object** (e.g. *the land, a story*) is usually a thing and the **indirect object** is usually a person (e.g. *the local people, the children*).
They gave ***the local people the land*** *back.* Or *They gave* ***the land*** *back* ***to the local people.***
The teacher read ***the children a story.*** Or *The teacher read* ***a story to the children.***
They saved ***us four seats.*** Or *They saved* ***four seats for us.***

- When we use a verb with two objects in the passive, there are also two possible structures.
  When we begin with the **direct object**, we use the preposition *to* or *for* before the **indirect object**.
  The local people *were given back* ***the land.*** Or ***The land*** *was given back* ***to the local people.***
  The children *were read* ***a story.*** Or ***A story*** *was read* ***to the children.***
  We *were saved* ***four seats.*** Or ***Four seats*** *were saved* ***for us.***

Verbs with two objects are: *award, buy, find, get, give, make, offer, promise, reserve, save, send, show.*

Examples

Tim Hogan ***was awarded*** *man-of-the-match.*
Man-of-the-match ***was awarded*** *to Tim Hogan.*
Has *Jack* ***been sent*** *the contract?*
Has *the contract* ***been sent*** *to Jack?*

G 7 Passive infinitive (with *to*) after *want, expect,* etc.

students' book, pages 24 – 25

Some verbs (e.g. *arrange, ask, expect, hope, need, plan, try, want, would like*) are followed by the *to*-infinitive. When there is a passive meaning, these verbs are followed by the passive infinitive (with *to*) (e.g. *to be met, to be invited*).
We didn't expect ***to be met*** *at the airport.*
I hope ***to be invited*** *to the opening ceremony.*
The battery needs ***to be charged*** *overnight.*
They had long wanted the site ***to be returned*** *to them.*

G 8 Passive infinitive (without *to*) after modal verbs

students' book, pages 24 – 25

Modal verbs (e.g. *can, will, must*) are followed by the infinitive (without *to*). When there is passive meaning, modal verbs are followed by the passive infinitive (without *to*) (e.g. *be seen, be opened, be invited*).
Ancient Aboriginal paintings ***can be seen*** *in caves in the rock.*
Some form of ID ***must be shown*** *when entering the building.*
The museum ***will be opened*** *by the Prime Minister.*
The new website ***might be launched*** *soon.*

Examples

Tasmania ***can be reached*** *by boat in about ten hours from Melbourne.*
This email address ***can't be used*** *for replies.*
You ***will be given*** *plenty of opportunity to visit galleries and exhibitions.*
You ***won't be contacted*** *unless you give us permission.*
Tickets for this museum ***must be booked*** *online.*
The flight ***might be delayed****.*

G 9 Reported speech in statements, questions, requests and orders (revision)

students' book, pages 28 – 29

<u>Statements</u>

- When reporting statements, we often use the past tense forms *said, told, mentioned, added, suggested*, etc. When we do this, we usually 'backshift' the tense (move the tense one step back in time) in the comment we are reporting. We also change the pronouns (*I* → *he / she, you* → *me, we* → *they*, etc.).

<u>Present tense</u>	→	<u>Past tense</u>
I'm *from Darwin.*		*She said she* ***was*** *from Darwin.*
We're having *a barbecue.*		*She mentioned they* ***were having*** *a barbecue.*
<u>Past tense / Present perfect</u>	→	<u>Past perfect</u>
Steve ***forgot*** *his phone.*		*She told me that Steve* ***had forgotten*** *his phone.*
We've *just* ***arrived****.*		*He said they'****d*** *just* ***arrived****.*
<u>*Will*</u>	→	<u>*Would*</u>
I'll *call you later.*		*She said she'****d*** *call me later.*
<u>*Can*</u>	→	<u>*Could*</u>
I ***can't*** *find the address.*		*He told me he* ***couldn't*** *find the address.*
<u>*Must*</u>	→	<u>*Had to*</u>
We ***must*** *leave.*		*She said they* ***had to*** *leave.*

- However, we sometimes use the past tense forms *said, told, mentioned*, etc. and do not change the tense. This is usually to show or make clear that something is still true, relevant or important.
Sam ***left*** *about an hour ago.* → *He mentioned that Sam* ***left*** *about an hour ago.*
I'll *be home in ten minutes.* → *She said she'****ll*** *be home in ten minutes.*

Questions

- When we report questions, we often use the past tense forms *asked, wanted to know, wondered, was wondering*, etc. We usually 'backshift' the tense in the question we are reporting.
  *Where **are** they **going**? → She wanted to know where they **were going**.*
  *What **did** you **buy**? → He was wondering what **I'd bought**.*

- However, we sometimes use the past tense forms *asked, wanted to know, was wondering*, etc. but do not change the tense. This is usually to show that something is still true, relevant or important.
  *Where's Jamie **going**? → She was wondering where Jamie**'s going**.*

- To report a *yes / no* question (without a question word) we use *if* or *whether.*
  *Are you a student? → He asked me **if** I was a student.*
  *Can you give me a surfing lesson? → Olga was wondering **whether** I could give her a surfing lesson.*

Note that the word order is different from direct questions.
*Where **does he live**? → She asked me where **he lived**.*
NOT ~~*She asked me where did he live*~~.
*When **are we leaving**? → He wanted to know when **we were leaving**.*
NOT ~~*He wanted to know when were we leaving.*~~

Requests and orders

- We can report a request with verbs such as *asked* and *wanted* + object + *to*-infinitive.
  *Could you repeat the question? → She asked **me to repeat** the question.*
  *Can you wait for me? → She wanted **us to wait** for her.*

- We can report an order with *told* + object + (*not*) *to*-infinitive.
  *You should apologize to them. → She told **me to apologize** to them.*
  *Don't be late again. → He told **me not to be** late again.*

Reporting verbs in a present tense

- We sometimes use a reporting verb in a present tense (e.g. *He says ..., She tells me ..., She's asked ..., Dave's suggesting ...*). In this case, the reported information stays in the same tense as the original comment.
  *It**'s** Jenna's birthday today. → Alice tells me it**'s** your birthday!*
  *We**'re going** to the beach. → Luke has just told me that they**'re going** to the beach.*
  *How long **has** she **lived** here? → She wants to know how long you**'ve lived** here.*

- We can also report requests and orders with a verb in a present tense.
  *Will you help me? → Gareth **wants** me to help him.*
  *Wait, please. → She**'s asked** us to wait.*

Examples

*He said he **was** from Wellington.*
*She said they **were going** to have a barbecue.*
*He asked me if I **was** OK.*
*Olga asked me if I **can give** her a surfing lesson.*
*He wanted to know where I **worked**.*
*Oliver wants me **to phone** him.*
*The receptionist asked us **to wait** a few minutes.*
*The teacher told the children **to be** quiet.*
*Oscar wants to know if you **can give** him a lift to the airport.*
*Magdalena tells me you**'re applying** for Australian citizenship.*

G 10 Changes to adverbs of time and place in reported speech

students' book, pages 28 – 29

When we are reporting, we sometimes need to change adverbs of time and place.
*I saw Anders **yesterday**. → She mentioned she'd seen Anders **the day before**.*
*I'll call you **next week**. → She said she'd call me **the following week**.*
*This is the first time I've been **here**. → He said it was the first time he'd been **there**.*

Common changes include:
yesterday → the day before
tomorrow → the next day / the day after
last weekend / week / month / year → the weekend / week / month / year before
next weekend / week / month / year → the following weekend / week / month / year
here → there

G 11 Gerunds and infinitives (revision)

students' book, pages 52 – 53

Sometimes we use two verbs together. When one verb follows another verb, the second verb is usually a gerund (*-ing*) or a *to*-infinitive.

- We use the gerund (*-ing*) after certain verbs. These include: *admit, avoid, deny, don't mind, enjoy, feel like, finish, imagine, look forward to, mention, miss, practise, prefer, recommend, risk, suggest.*
  *Many young people **enjoy travelling** and want to volunteer abroad.*
  *Have you **finished reading** the article?*
  *He **suggests doing** work experience at a law firm.*

- We use the *to*-infinitive after certain verbs. These include: *arrange, choose, decide, expect, hope, intend, learn, manage, need, offer, plan, promise, want, would like.*
  *She's **decided to study** music at university.*
  *Many young people enjoy travelling and **want to volunteer** abroad.*
  ***I'd like to do** some kind of volunteer work.*

- Some verbs can be followed by the gerund or the *to*-infinitive with no or little difference in meaning. These include: *like, love, hate, prefer, start.*
  *I **hate getting up** early.* *I really **hate to be** late.*
  *I **prefer doing** sport.* *I **prefer to study** languages.*

Some verbs can be followed by a gerund or the *to*-infinitive but there is a difference in meaning. These include: *try, remember, forget, stop.*

- *Try*
  We use *try* + gerund when we do something to see what the results will be.
  *I **tried turning** the computer on and off, but the program still didn't work.*

  We use *try* + *to*-infinitive when we make an effort to achieve something.
  *I'm **trying to learn** Russian, but it's very difficult.*

- <u>*Remember* and *forget*</u>
  We use *remember / forget* + gerund to talk about memories.
  *Do you **remember going** to school for the first time?*
  *I'll never **forget visiting** Prague. It's so beautiful.*

  We use *remember / forget* + *to*-infinitive to say we do or don't do something.
  *Did you **remember to email** Julia?*
  *Don't **forget to update** your CV!*

- <u>*Stop*</u>
  We use *stop* + gerund to talk about something ending or stopping.
  *I **stopped eating** meat when I was 16.*

  We use *stop* + *to*-infinitive to express the reason or purpose.
  *I was working, but I **stopped to check** the news for a while.*

G 12 Expressing the future (revision)

students' book, pages 52 – 53

<u>*Will* for decisions and predictions</u>

- We use *will* for spontaneous decisions. This includes offers, promises and requests.
  *We've got a free hour or so. I think **I'll do** some sightseeing.*
  *Are you ready to order? – Yes, **I'll have** the vegetarian pizza, please.*
  ***I'll help** you with the cooking if you like.*

- We use *will* for predictions that are based on personal feeling or opinion.
  *I am sure **you'll have** a great time in Australia.*
  *Based on my work so far, **I'll be** OK.*
  *They **won't win.** We're a much better team.*

<u>*Be going to* for future plans</u>

- We use *be going to* for future plans and intentions.
  ***I'm going to ask** for a pay rise.*
  *James **is going to book** his plane tickets at the weekend.*
  ***Are** you **going to apply for** the job?*

Note that to avoid repeating *go*, we often omit *to go*.
*We**'re going** (to go) shopping this evening.*
*My best friend and I **are going** (to go) to Australia for the summer.*

<u>Simple present with future meaning</u>

- We use the simple present to talk about events in the future that are part of a fixed timetable, itinerary or programme.
  *In March, I **have** an interview for a job. It's on the 16th.*
  *The apprenticeship **starts** in September.*
  *The doors **open** at 6.30 and the show **starts** at 7.30.*
  *The flight **leaves** at 11.00. When **does** it **arrive** in Perth?*

Present progressive with future meaning

- We use the present progressive with a future time to talk about future arrangements.
  *Next week, I**'m meeting** my cousin to talk things through.*
  *I**'m seeing** my friends tomorrow evening. We**'re going** for a pizza.*
  *Did you know that Michael**'s having** a party next Saturday?*
  *When **are** Chris and Jo **getting married**?*

Future perfect

- We use the future perfect (*will have* + past participle) to talk about something already completed at a point in the future.
  *The apprenticeship starts in September. I**'ll have finished** my A-levels by then.*
  *I'm sure we**'ll have arrived** by midnight.*
  ***Will** you **have had** dinner by 8.30?*

- We can use the future perfect to talk about something not completed at a point in the future.
  *I'm afraid I **won't have finished** my report by Friday.*
  *I **won't have had** time to do much research before the interview.*

- We often use the future perfect with *by.*
  *We'll have finished the meeting **by** 10.30.*

G 13 Future progressive

students' book, pages 52 – 53

- We form the future progressive with *will be* + *-ing*.
  *We**'ll be travelling** all day.*
  *I**'ll be waiting** when you arrive.*

- We use the future progressive for something in progress at a specific time in the future.
  *Next year most of my friends **will be doing** a university course or an apprenticeship.*
  *Hopefully by September I**'ll be working** somewhere in the US or Canada.*
  *This time tomorrow, I**'ll be having** my interview.*
  *At 3 o'clock, we**'ll be driving** to the airport.*

G 14 Modal verbs (revision)

students' book, pages 56 – 57

The modal verbs are *can, could, must, might, may, would, will, shall* and *should.*

- A modal verb always has the same form. The ending never changes.
  *She **can** speak English.*

- We use an infinitive without *to* after a modal verb.
  *I **will** help you.*

- To form a question, we put the modal verb before the subject.
  ***Can** you help me?*

- To form a negative, we put *not* or *n't* after the modal verb.
  *You **mustn't** do that.*

Can and *could*

We use *can* to talk about ability. We use it:

- to talk about general abilities and skills.
  *Amir **can** use many computer programs.*
  *I **can** speak French and Spanish. But I **can't** speak Italian.*

- to talk about ability at a particular time.
  *I **can't** read this. The writing is too small.*

The past tense of *can* is *could*.
*I **could** speak some English when I was four years old.*

We use *can* to talk about permission. We use it:

- to talk about rules and laws and permission given by an individual.
  *You **can't** wear trainers at work. But you **can** wear jeans.*
  *You **can** leave when you have finished the report.*

The past tense of *can* is *could*.
*We **could** wear trainers at work in my last job.*

We use *can* to talk about possibility.
*We **can** have the meeting on Thursday or Friday.*
*A cover letter **can** help you sell your skills and knowledge.*

May and *might*

We use *may* and *might* to say that something is possible or likely. *Might* is more common in informal contexts. The negative is *may not* and *might not*. We use them:

- to say what is possible or likely in the future.
  *I **might** start looking for a new job.*
  *There **may** be a slight delay with your order.*

- to say what we think is possible or likely in the present.
  *This **might** be Nina's office. But I'm not sure.*
  *She didn't answer the phone. She **might not** be at home.*

Must

We use *must* to talk about what is necessary or what is required. We use *must not* (or *mustn't*) to say that something is not allowed or forbidden.
*Education and work experience details **must** be included in your CV.*
*You **mustn't** be late for your interview!*

Should

We use *should* to make suggestions and give advice. The negative form is *shouldn't*.
*Your CV **should** have a clear format and structure.*
*You **shouldn't** invent information in your CV.*

The past tense of *should* is *should have* + past participle.
*We're going to be late – we **should have left** earlier.*

<u>*Will* and *shall*</u>

We use *will* in a number of ways. Note that *will* is often contracted to *'ll*. We use *will*:

- to express spontaneous decisions.
  *I'**ll** help you if you want me to.*
  *I think I'**ll** take a short break.*

- to express predictions or assumptions about the future, present or past.
  *I'm hoping I'**ll** finish the report by Friday.*
  *Hurry up! The taxi **will** be waiting.*
  *I think the meeting **will** have finished by now.*

- to talk about facts we see as inevitable or certain.
  *I'**ll** be at work all day tomorrow.*
  *She'**ll** be 21 in January.*
  *No hiring manager **will** be willing to consider your application.*

We mainly use *shall* in the form of a question to make offers and suggestions. We use it in this way with *I* and *we*.
***Shall** I help you?*
*What time **shall** we meet?*

G 15 Modal substitutes

students' book, pages 56 – 57

Modal substitutes include: *be able to, have to, need to, be obliged to, ought to* and *be supposed to*.

<u>Alternatives to *can* and *could*</u>

- We use *be able to* as an alternative to *can* and *could*. This is usually in more formal contexts and with *will* and the present perfect.
  *Some people **are able to** speak several languages.*
  ***I'm** not **able to** fix the problem, I'm afraid.*
  *Unfortunately, I **wasn't able to** find his office.*
  *With her CV, I think she'**ll be able to** get an apprenticeship.*
  ***I've been able to** speak English since I was four.*

- We can sometimes use *be allowed to* as an alternative to *can* and *could* to talk about permission.
  ***Are** you **allowed to** wear jeans at work?*
  *I **was** never **allowed to** stay up late on a school night.*

<u>Alternatives to *must*</u>

- We use *need to* and *have to* as alternatives to *must*. When they are used in this way, there is usually little difference in meaning (e.g. *I **need to** prepare for my interview. / I **have to** prepare for my interview. / I **must** prepare for my interview.*).
  *You **need to** show some ID to get into the building.*
  *You **need to** leave by 5.30 at the latest.*
  *Do you **have to** wear a tie at work?*

- In more informal contexts, such as conversation, we can use *have got to*.
  ***I've got to** prepare for my interview.*
  *What time **have** we **got to** leave?*

- The past tenses are *needed to* and *had to*. We use *had to* as the past tense of *must*.
  *Sorry I'm late. I **needed to** stop at the shops on the way here.*
  *I **had to** stay at work later than usual today.*
  *He **had to** do an interview with the manager.*

- We use *don't need to* and *don't have to* to say that something isn't necessary.
  *We **don't need to** leave until midday.*
  *In some countries, you **don't have to** give personal details in your CV.*

- We use *be obliged to* as an alternative in more formal contexts. This is usually when the obligation is a rule or law.
  *You **are obliged to** report to the reception on arrival and when leaving the building.*
  *In the UK, you **are not obliged to** add a headshot photo.*

<u>Alternatives to *should*</u>

- We can sometimes use *ought to* as an alternative to *should* when we are making suggestions or giving advice.
  *If you have skills, awards or other achievements, you **ought to** highlight them here.*
  *You **ought to** wear a tie for the interview.*
  *I think we **ought to** leave now.*

- We use *be supposed to* as an alternative to *should* when we are expressing the correct thing to do.
  ***Are** we **supposed to** include our age in our CV?*
  *In some European countries you**'re supposed to** include this information.*

Examples

*I **wasn't able to** get there in time, I'm afraid.*
***Will** you **be able to** fix it, do you think?*
*I **might be able to** go on the visit, but I'm not sure.*
***I've got to** finish this report.*
*What time **do** we **need to** leave?*
*I **had to** work late last night.*
*We **don't have to** go to the meeting. But you can if you want to.*
*The meeting **ought to** take about an hour.*

G 16 *make, let, allow*

students' book, pages 62 – 63

Verb phrases with *make*, *let*, *allow* + object + infinitive can often be expressed with 'lassen' or 'veranlassen' in German.
The sudden noise ***made him scream****. (Das plötzliche Geräusch ließ ihn aufschreien.)*

- We use *make* + object + infinitive (without *to*).
  Technological advances have ***made us reassess*** *our work-life balance.*
  No one can ***make you do*** *anything you don't want to do.*

- We use *let* + object + infinitive (without *to*).
  Specialized apps ***let you choose*** *when and where you want to work.*
  A freelance career ***lets you set*** *your own hours.*

- We use *allow* + object + *to*-infinitive.
  The gig economy ***allows you to plan*** *your own work schedule and be more independent.*
  Freelancer platforms ***allow you to bid*** *for jobs that match your skills.*

G 17 *have something done*

students' book, pages 62 – 63

- We use *have something done* to say that someone does something for us. This is usually when we have arranged it, often when it is some kind of service. The form is *have* + object + past participle.
  Many people ***have groceries delivered*** *to their home.*
  We ***had the office decorated*** *last month.*
  I'm having my hair cut *tomorrow.*

- We can also use *get something done*. This is generally in more informal contexts, such as a conversation.
  We ***get the car serviced*** *every year.*
  Where do you ***get your hair cut****?*

G 18 *used to / didn't use to / would*

students' book, pages 62 – 63

Used to
We use *used to* + infinitive to talk about past actions or situations that no longer exist. This could be:

- past actions, habits and routines
  My dad ***used to spend*** *an hour a day commuting to work.*
  I ***didn't use to drive*** *to work, but these days I usually do.*
  Do you work in advertising? – No, but I ***used to****.*

- past states
  The manufacturing industry ***used to be*** *the biggest employer.*
  The workplace ***didn't use to be*** *as stressful as today.*
  There ***used to be*** *a cinema here.*

Note that there is no final '*d*' in negatives and questions.
There ***didn't use to be*** *so many service industries here.*
What ***did*** *people* ***use to do*** *before mobile phones?*

<u>*Would*</u>

- We can also use *would* + infinitive to talk about past actions, habits and routines. *Would* is usually contracted to *'d* after pronouns.
  In the past, workers ***would travel*** *to their workplace every day.*
  Employees ***would commute*** *to the office every day.*
  *In my old job, we****'d have*** *a meeting almost every day.*

- We do not, however, use *would* to talk about past states.
  NOT ~~*The manufacturing industry would be the biggest employer.*~~

Examples

We ***used to live*** *in Frankfurt.*
I ***used to cycle*** *to school every day.*
There ***used to be*** *a lovely park here.*
Didn't *there* ***use to be*** *an office here?*
*As a child, I****'d spend*** *hours playing computer games.*
*We****'d often stay up*** *all night when we were students.*

G 19 Participle constructions

students' book, pages 66 – 67

There are two main types of participle:

- the present participle (the *-ing* form of the verb)
  Before ***arriving,*** *I received lots of information.*
  Wanting *to become a teacher, he volunteered at his local school.*

- the past participle (the regular *-ed* form or an irregular form).
  If ***asked,*** *I would do it again.*
  I came across a fantastic organization, ***run*** *by an Irish government agency.*

We also use the perfect participle (e.g. *having done*).
Having spent *eight wonderful weeks there, I can thoroughly recommend it.*

To form the negative, we put *not* or *never* before the participle.
Not wanting *to be late, they set off in plenty of time.*
Never having been *to Ireland before, I was determined to see as much as I could.*

We can use present participle constructions:

- in clauses beginning with *before, after, while, since, when*, etc.
  Before arriving, *I received lots of information. (= Before I arrived, I received lots of information.)*
  I came across InternIreland ***while researching internships abroad.***
  After filling in an online application, *I was invited to a 30-minute video interview.*
  She's worked here ***since finishing university.***

- when we express the reason for an action:
  Feeling tired, *he left work early. (= Because he felt tired, he left work early.)*
  Wanting to get as much experience as possible, *I didn't mind having to work some weekends.*
  Not earning much *at the factory, he took a second job working in a café.*

Note that in the above present participle constructions, the subject of both clauses is the same person.

- in reduced relative clauses when we shorten a defining relative clause, for example:
  in progressive tenses when we remove the relative pronoun and *be* or in place of a relative pronoun + simple tense to express a fact, state or permanent situation.
  Who are the people ***talking to Harry****? (= Who are the people who are talking to Harry?)*
  I work in an office ***overlooking the river****. (= I work in an office that overlooks the river.)*

We can use perfect participle constructions when one event happens before another event. We use the perfect participle to emphasize that the first event is completed before the second or that there is a time interval between the two events.
Having finished *all their exams, they organized a big party.*
Having overslept, *she was late for work.*

Note that beginning a sentence with a participle clause is more common in more formal writing and literary contexts.

We can use past participle constructions:

- in reduced defining or non-defining relative clauses. We remove the relative pronoun and the verb *be* in passive structure.
  It's a local business, ***run*** *by the same family for over 200 years. (= It's a local business, which has been run by the same family for over 200 years.)*
  Have they found the money ***stolen*** *from the office?*
  Cars ***parked*** *here will be removed.*

- in shortened *if* clauses to give passive meaning. We can include *if* or leave out *if.*
  If ***asked*** *about it, I'd say it was the prettiest place I've visited so far. (= If I was asked about it, ...)*
  Given *the chance to take the exam again, I'd do it without hesitation. (= If I was given the chance, ...)*

Examples
After leaving *university, he got a job in a bank.*
Living alone, *Fred always looked forward to the few visitors he had.*
Having *suddenly* ***quit*** *his job, he needed to look for something else.*
Having passed *all my exams, I felt quite pleased with myself.*
Bags ***left*** *unattended will be destroyed.*
Given *the chance, I'd love to live abroad for a year or two.*

G 20 Defining and non-defining relative clauses (revision)

students' book, pages 90 – 91

Relative pronouns
We use *who* for people and *which* for things. We can use *that* for both people and things. We use *whose* to show possession.

Defining relative clauses
A defining relative clause defines, identifies or gives necessary information about a person or thing. A defining relative clause comes immediately after this person or thing. The relative clause begins with a relative pronoun.
The traditional nuclear family ***that consists of two married parents and their children*** *is no longer the standard.*
Kids ***who came over*** *would sometimes ask, 'Where's your dad?'*
Is this the book ***which your parents gave you as a birthday gift****?*
Mac and his family do things ***that every other family does.***
This is my friend ***whose paintings I showed you.***

Omission of the relative pronoun
A relative pronoun can be the subject or the object of a relative clause.

	relative pronoun / subject	verb	object	
There's the man	***who***	*helped*	*us*	*yesterday.*

	relative pronoun / object	subject	verb	
There's the man	***who***	*we*	*helped*	*yesterday.*

We can omit *who, which* or *that* when it is the object of the relative clause.
There's the man (who) we helped yesterday.
Is this the book (which) your parents gave you as a birthday gift?
Mac and his family do things (that) every other family does.
Is this the café (that) Luke mentioned the other day?
NOT ~~*There's the man helped us yesterday.*~~

Non-defining relative clauses
A non-defining relative clause gives extra non-essential information about a person or thing. The non-defining relative clause comes immediately after this person or thing and begins with *who* or *which,* but not *that*. We always separate a non-defining relative clause from the main clause with commas.
Same-sex marriage, ***which was legalized in Canada in 2005,*** *has led to even more diversity.*
Single-parent families, ***which can be a single mum or a dad plus kids,*** *are not unusual.*
My two older brothers, ***who I've always been very close to,*** *went to live with my dad.*
My best friend, ***whose parents divorced when she was a baby,*** *was brought up by her mum.*
He was born in Avalon, ***which is a small town near Los Angeles.***

Note that non-defining relative clauses are used more in writing and in more formal spoken contexts.

We can also use a non-defining relative clause beginning with *which* to comment on the whole of the previous clause.
I was at a party last weekend, ***which was great fun****.*
The school became mixed-sex in the 1980s, ***which was a major step forwards.***
I missed the bus, ***which was really annoying****.*

Note that non-defining relative clauses used to comment on the whole of the previous clause are quite common in spoken and more informal English.

Where and *when*
We can use the relative adverbs *where* and *when* in relative clauses. We use *where* to identify a place and *when* to identify a time.
The hotel ***where we stayed*** *is in the city centre.*
Thanksgiving is a day ***when families and friends get together****.*
Carmel, ***where we went the other week,*** *is one of my favourite places.*

Examples

The friend ***who you met the other day*** *is a lawyer.*
The couple ***that live in the flat above us*** *are very noisy.*
What's that game ***we were playing*** *last night?*
Mr Jones, ***who also actually taught my mum,*** *is my maths teacher.*
Christmas is usually a time ***when families come together****.*
Maria offered to help, ***which was very kind of her****.*

G 21 Participle constructions replacing relative clauses

students' book, pages 90 – 91

A relative clause can be shortened using a present or past participle.

- When the relative pronoun is followed by the verb *be*, we can usually omit both the relative pronoun and *be*.
  Who are the people ***talking*** *to Erica? (= Who are the people* ***who are talking*** *to Erica?)*
  Canada is a nation ***composed*** *mostly of immigrants. (= Canada is a nation* ***which is composed*** *mostly of immigrants.)*

- We can sometimes use a present participle in place of a relative pronoun and simple tense. This is when we express a fact, state or permanent situation.
  The traditional nuclear family ***consisting of*** *two married parents and their children is no longer the standard.* (= *The traditional nuclear family* ***which consists*** *of two married parents and their children is no longer the standard.*)
  The majority of people ***living*** *in Canada are originally from elsewhere.* (= *The majority of people* ***who live*** *in Canada are originally from elsewhere.*)

Examples

We stayed in a hotel ***overlooking*** *the main square.*
Bags ***left*** *unattended will be removed.*
The people ***living*** *next door are very friendly.*

G 22 *be used to / get used to* + noun / *-ing*

students' book, pages 90 – 91

- The verb phrase *be used to* means being familiar with something.
  *I've lived here for a few years, so **I'm used to the weather**.*
  *Valerie's grandmother **wasn't used to living alone**.*
  ***I'm not used to driving on the right**. I'm from the UK.*

- The verb phrase *get used to* describes the process of becoming familiar with something.
  *Immigrants have to **get used to a new culture** and new customs.*
  *I'm finally **getting used to the Canadian way of life**.*
  *Children in blended families have to **get used to living in a new unit**.*

Note that *be / get used to* is followed by a noun or the *-ing* form of a verb.

Examples

*I'**m not used to speaking** English all day.*
*I didn't take me long to **get used to the Canadian accent**.*
***Are** you **getting used to the way of life** here?*

G 23 Emphatic *do / does / did*

students' book, pages 94 – 95

We can use a form of the auxiliary verb *do* (*do / does / did*) to give emphasis to a statement.
In speaking, we stress *do / does / did*. We use *do* in this way for two reasons:

- to emphasize our feelings or emotions
  *Maybe it was a silly reaction, but it **did** make my life easier.*
  *At school a lot of kids dress alike, so we **do** influence each other.*
  *Anna **does** have some great ideas, don't you think?*
  *I **do** like Mexican food, especially the spicier dishes.*

- to emphasize a contrast
  *We didn't get caught ourselves, but a kid from our school **did**.*
  *I don't do any sport, but I **do** like watching it on TV.*
  *He doesn't drive, but he **does** have a motorbike licence.*

Note that with tenses and forms that already have an auxiliary verb, in speaking we stress the auxiliary verb to express emphasis in a similar way.
*I **am** looking forward to the party next weekend.*
*We really **have** had a great time, thank you.*

Examples

*I **do** agree with you. Please believe me!*
*The new sports centre **does** have an amazing offer.*
*My friend didn't like it, but I **did** enjoy the film.*

G 24 Emphatic pronouns with *-self / -selves*

students' book, pages 94 – 95

The reflexive pronouns *myself, yourself, himself, herself, itself, ourselves, yourselves* and *themselves* can also be used for emphasis.

- We can use them after a verb to emphasize the person or thing that does the action.
  *I knew **myself** that it was wrong.*
  *We didn't get caught **ourselves**, but a kid from our school did.*
  *He admitted **himself** that it was wrong.*
- They can also occur directly after the subject or subject pronoun.
  *Alex **herself** invited me to the party.*
  *You **yourself** created the problem, I'm afraid.*

G 25 *If*-sentences type 2 and 3 (revision)

students' book, pages 100 – 101

If-sentences type 2

- We use *if*-sentences type 2 to talk about things that are impossible or hypothetical in the present or unlikely to happen in the future.
- *If*-sentences type 2 have the form *if* + simple past, *would / wouldn't* + infinitive.
  *If I **was** over 18, I **would** definitely **go** to jail.*
  *If we **drove** less, there **wouldn't be** so much air pollution.*
  *If I **had** more money, I'**d buy** a new phone.*

Note that we often use *'d* instead of *would*, especially in speaking and informal writing.

- We do not use *would* in the *if*-clause.
  *If I **had** more time, I'd read more books.* NOT ~~*If I would have more time, I'd read more books.*~~
- We can usually swap the order of the two clauses. When the *if* clause is first, there is a comma between the clauses.
  *If I had more time**,** I'd read more books.* *I'd read more books if I had more time.*
- We can usually use *If I was* ... or *If I were* ... . However, we normally use *If I were you, ...* .
  *If I **was / were** richer, I'd get a new car.*
  ***If I were you**, I'd work a bit harder at school.*

Note that we can use *could* or *might* in an *if*-sentence type 2.
*If I had more money, I **could buy** a new phone.*
*If we drove less, there **might not be** so much air pollution.*

If-sentences type 3

- We use *if*-sentences type 3 to talk about something that didn't happen in the past. We talk about it in an imaginary or a hypothetical way.
- *If*-sentences type 3 have the form *if* + past perfect, *would / wouldn't have* + past participle.
  *If the road **hadn't been** icy, I **wouldn't have lost** control of the car.*
  *If Jake **hadn't taken** his sister's car, the accident **wouldn't have happened**.*
  *If you'**d got up** earlier, you **wouldn't have missed** the bus.*

- We often use *'d* instead of *had* and *would*, especially in speaking and informal writing. We also often use *'ve* instead of *have*.
  *If I'**d had** more money, I'**d've got** a taxi.*

- We can usually swap the order of the two clauses. When the *if* clause is first, there is a comma between the clauses.
  If I'd had more money, I would've bought it. *I would've bought it if I'd had more money.*

Note that we can use *could have* or *might have* in an *if*-sentence type 3.
*If I hadn't been ill last week, I **could have gone** to the meeting.*
*If I'd worked harder, I **might've got** better grades in my exams.*

Examples
*If I **had** more time, I'**d help** you.*
*What **would** you **do** if you **found** a wallet in the street?*
*If I **was** richer, I'**d buy** a sports car and drive round Europe for a year!*
*If I'**d had** more time, I'**d have been able to** help you.*
*If we'**d left** earlier, we'**d have missed** the terrible traffic.*

G 26 *If*-sentences mixed conditionals

students' book, pages 100 – 101

We use a 'mixed' conditional to talk about a past event with a present consequence. To do this we combine a type 3-conditional (to refer to the past) with a type-2 conditional (to refer to the present).

*If Jake **hadn't been** so stupid, he **wouldn't be** in court now.*
*If you'**d listened** to the advice, you **wouldn't be** in this mess now.*
*If you'**d gone** to bed earlier last night, you **wouldn't be** so tired now.*
*He'**d be** at university now if he **hadn't failed** his exams.*

Note that we can use *might* in a mixed conditional sentence.
*If you'd listened to the advice, you **might not be** in this mess now.*

G 27 Using *It* … and *What* … for emphasis

students' book, pages 104 – 105

We can use sentences beginning with *It* ... or *What* ... to give emphasis to what we are saying. This helps to focus attention on or 'spotlights' the important information.

Neutral sentence	→	Sentence with emphasis
I didn't delete the files.		***It wasn't** me **who** deleted the files.*
All the advertising annoys me.		***What** annoys me **is** all the advertising.*

The main forms are:
- ***It is / was … that / who / which …***
  ***It's** all the advertising **which** annoys me.*
  ***It's** the advertisers **who** want our money.*
  ***It's** the video ads **that** really catch your attention.*
  ***It was** Jenny **who** phoned, not Maria.*

- ***What** … **is** / **are** / **was** / **were** …*
  ***What** it means **is** that we enjoy clever content, even if it's advertising.*
  ***What** is really annoying **are** those ads blocking the content.*
  ***What** we needed **was** a better internet connection.*
  ***What** we needed **were** more options to choose from.*

Examples

***It was** clicking on the ad **that** caused the virus.*
***It wasn't** Masha **who** phoned, it was Olga.*
***Was it** Professor Jones **who** retired last month?*
***What I** don't understand **is** why no one said anything to her.*
***What** annoys me **is** his lazy attitude.*

G 28 Using inversion to make a text more formal

students' book, pages 104 – 105

In more formal contexts, we can sometimes start a sentence with a negative adverbial such as *Hardly ever …, Rarely …, Never …, Not once …, In no way …, Only later, …*, etc. We do this to give emphasis or for dramatic effect. Compare the following sentences:

Neutral sentence →	Sentence with emphasis
You rarely see a website with no advertising.	***Rarely** do you see a website with no advertising.*
I haven't once sold advertising space.	***Not once** have I sold advertising space.*

Note that when we start a sentence with a negative adverbial, we change the word order: the **auxiliary verb** is before the **subject**. In the simple present, we add the auxiliary *do* or *does*; in the simple past *did*.

***Rarely do you** see a website with no advertising.* NOT ~~*Rarely you see a website with no advertising.*~~
***Not once have I** sold advertising space.* NOT ~~*Not once I have sold advertising space.*~~

Examples

***In no way am I** saying all advertising is bad.*
***Rarely do I** take any notice of banner ads.*
***Never before have I** heard such stupidity.*
***Hardly ever does such an opportunity** arise.*
***At no time did I** say that.*
***Not once, did he** apologize.*
***Only later, did we** realize we'd made such a terrible mistake.*

Irregular verbs

infinitive	simple past	past participle	German
to **be**	**was / were**	**been**	sein
to **beat**	**beat**	**beaten**	schlagen
to **become**	**became**	**become**	werden
to **begin**	**began**	**begun**	beginnen, anfangen
to **bet**	**bet**	**bet**	wetten
to **bite** [baɪt]	**bit** [bɪt]	**bitten** ['bɪtn]	beißen
to **blow**	**blew**	**blown**	blasen
to **break**	**broke**	**broken**	brechen
to **bring**	**brought**	**brought**	bringen
to **build**	**built**	**built**	bauen
to **burn**	**burnt / burned**	**burnt / burned**	(ver)brennen
to **buy**	**bought**	**bought**	kaufen
to **catch**	**caught**	**caught**	fangen
to **choose** [uː]	**chose** [əʊ]	**chosen** [əʊ]	auswählen
to **come**	**came**	**come**	kommen
to **cost**	**cost**	**cost**	kosten
to **cut**	**cut**	**cut**	schneiden
to **deal** [diːl]	**dealt** [delt]	**dealt** [delt]	handeln
to **dig**	**dug**	**dug**	graben
to **do**	**did**	**done** [dʌn]	machen, tun
to **draw**	**drew**	**drawn**	zeichnen
to **dream**	**dreamt / dreamed** [dremt]	**dreamt / dreamed** [dremt]	träumen
to **drink**	**drank**	**drunk**	trinken
to **drive**	**drove**	**driven**	fahren
to **eat**	**ate**	**eaten**	essen
to **fall**	**fell**	**fallen**	fallen, stürzen
to **feed** [fiːd]	**fed** [fed]	**fed** [fed]	füttern
to **feel** [fiːl]	**felt** [felt]	**felt** [felt]	(sich) fühlen, spüren
to **fight**	**fought**	**fought**	kämpfen
to **find**	**found**	**found**	finden
to **fly**	**flew**	**flown**	fliegen
to **forget**	**forgot**	**forgotten**	vergessen
to **forgive**	**forgave**	**forgiven**	vergeben
to **freeze**	**froze**	**frozen**	frieren
to **get**	**got**	**got / gotten** (AE)	bekommen, holen
to **give**	**gave**	**given**	geben, schenken
to **go**	**went**	**gone**	gehen, fahren
to **grow**	**grew**	**grown**	wachsen, anbauen
to **hang**	**hung**	**hung**	hängen
to **have (got)**	**had**	**had**	haben
to **hear** [ɪə]	**heard** [ɜː]	**heard** [ɜː]	hören
to **hide** [haɪd]	**hid** [hɪd]	**hidden** [hɪdn]	(sich) verstecken
to **hit**	**hit**	**hit**	schlagen
to **hold**	**held**	**held**	halten
to **hurt**	**hurt**	**hurt**	wehtun
to **keep** [kiːp]	**kept** [kept]	**kept** [kept]	(be)halten
to **kneel** [niːl]	**knelt** [nelt]	**knelt** [nelt]	knien
to **know** [nəʊ]	**knew** [njuː]	**known** [nəʊn]	wissen, kennen
to **lead** [liːd]	**led** [led]	**led** [led]	führen
to **learn**	**learnt / learned**	**learnt / learned**	lernen
to **leave**	**left**	**left**	verlassen
to **lend**	**lent**	**lent**	leihen

infinitive	simple past	past participle	German
to **let**	**let**	**let**	lassen
to **lie**	**lay**	**lain**	liegen
to **light**	**lit / lighted**	**lit / lighted**	anzünden, anmachen
to **lose** [uː]	**lost** [ɒ]	**lost** [ɒ]	verlieren
to **make**	**made**	**made**	machen, herstellen
to **mean** [iː]	**meant** [e]	**meant** [e]	bedeuten
to **meet** [miːt]	**met** [met]	**met** [met]	(sich) treffen, kennen-lernen
to **mow**	**mowed**	**mown / mowed**	mähen
to **pay**	**paid**	**paid**	bezahlen
to **put**	**put**	**put**	stellen
to **quit**	**quit**	**quit**	aufhören
to **read** [iː]	**read** [e]	**read** [e]	lesen
to **rebuild**	**rebuilt**	**rebuilt**	wieder aufbauen
to **rewrite**	**rewrote**	**rewritten**	umschreiben
to **ride**	**rode**	**ridden**	fahren, reiten
to **ring**	**rang**	**rung**	klingeln, anrufen
to **rise**	**rose**	**risen**	ansteigen, (sich) erheben
to **run**	**ran**	**run**	laufen, rennen, leiten
to **say**	**said**	**said**	sagen
to **see**	**saw**	**seen**	sehen
to **sell**	**sold**	**sold**	verkaufen
to **send**	**sent**	**sent**	schicken
to **set**	**set**	**set**	setzen, stellen, legen
to **shake**	**shook**	**shaken**	schütteln
to **shine**	**shone**	**shone**	scheinen

infinitive	simple past	past participle	German
to **shoot** [ʃuːt]	**shot** [ʃɒt]	**shot** [ʃɒt]	schießen
to **show**	**showed**	**shown / showed**	zeigen
to **sing**	**sang**	**sung**	singen
to **sink**	**sank**	**sunk**	sinken
to **sit**	**sat**	**sat**	sitzen
to **sleep** [sliːp]	**slept** [slept]	**slept** [slept]	schlafen
to **smell**	**smelt / smelled**	**smelt / smelled**	riechen
to **speak**	**spoke**	**spoken**	sprechen
to **spend**	**spent**	**spent**	verbringen, ausgeben
to **split**	**split**	**split**	sich trennen
to **spoil**	**spoilt**	**spoilt**	verderben
to **spread**	**spread**	**spread**	(sich) ausbreiten
to **stand**	**stood**	**stood**	stehen
to **steal**	**stole**	**stolen**	stehlen
to **stick**	**stuck**	**stuck**	kleben
to **sting**	**stung**	**stung**	stechen
to **swim**	**swam**	**swum**	schwimmen
to **take**	**took**	**taken**	nehmen, dauern
to **teach**	**taught**	**taught**	unterrichten
to **tell**	**told**	**told**	sagen, erzählen
to **think**	**thought**	**thought**	denken, glauben
to **throw**	**threw**	**thrown**	werfen
to **understand**	**understood**	**understood**	verstehen
to **wake up**	**woke up**	**woken up**	aufwachen, aufwecken
to **wear**	**wore**	**worn**	tragen
to **win**	**won** [ʌ]	**won**	gewinnen
to **write**	**wrote**	**written**	schreiben

Acknowledgements

Text credits

S. 17: "Closing The Gap: Australia's indigenous inequality 'not good enough'", BBC, 12. Februar 2020, https://www.bbc.com/news/world-australia-51469708; "Aboriginal Australian's 'still suffering effects of colonial past'", Shaimaa Khalil, BBC 16. Juli 2020, https://www.bbc.com/news/world-australia-53436225; **S. 22:** "Why is Australia a global leader in wildlife extinctions?", Mike Foley, The Sydney Morning Herald, 20. Juli 2020, https://www.smh.com.au/politics/federal/why-is-australia-a-global-leader-in-wildlife-extinctions-20200717-p55cyd.html; "Australia confirms extinction of 13 more species, including first reptile since colonisation", Adam Morton, The Guardian, 3. März 2021, https://www.theguardian.com/science/2021/mar/03/australia-confirms-extinction-of-13-more-species-including-first-reptile-since-colonisation, "'Really depressing': National environment laws failing to deliver", Mike Foley, 14. Juni 2020, https://www.smh.com.au/politics/federal/really-depressing-national-environment-laws-failing-to-deliver-20200610-p551fs.html; **S. 30:** "Australien in 100 Tagen – Der Kinofilm: Blu-ray", Christian Wüstenberg, comfilm.de, https://comfilm.de/Australien-in-100-Tagen-Der-Kinofilm-Blu-ray; **S. 55:** "Bis zu 1900 Prozent Rendite – das Geschäft mit dem 'weißen Gold' vom Golfplatz", Felix Eick, WELT, 29. September 2020, https://www.welt.de/wirtschaft/karriere/article216747978/Professioneller-Golfballtaucher-Bis-zu-1900-Prozent-Rendite-mit-weissem-Gold.html; **S. 56:** "The 20 Most Extraordinary Jobs in the World", James Ball, https://www.coburgbanks.co.uk/blog/friday-funnies/20-most-extraordinary-jobs/; **S. 80:** "Vegetarische Ernährung – wie gesund ist sie?", AOK Gesundheitsmagazin, https://www.aok.de/pk/magazin/ernaehrung/ernaehrungsformen/vegetarische-ernaehrung-wie-gesund-ist-sie/

Picture credits

|Alamy Stock Photo, Abingdon/Oxfordshire: AFPhoto 90.1; amanda rose 46.1; anton havelaar 41.2; Artokoloro 14.1; Christoph & Friends/Das Fotoarchiv 91.1; Craddock, Samantha 103.1; creativephototeam 99.1; Daisy-Daisy 63.1; dave cooil 86.1; david hancock 17.2; Delphotos 51.1; Dolgachov, Lev 97.1; Fernandez, Antonio Guillem 38.1, 62.1, 65.1; Gina Easley/Stockimo 41.3; Glasshouse Images 44.1; infinity 22.1; insta_photos 75.1; Jemastock 52.1; Lightboxx 25.1; Lusiyk, Vira 95.1; Maridav 87.1; MBI 102.1; Panther Media GmbH 106.1; Popov, Andriy 53.1; Prostock-studio 56.1; rico ploeg 41.1; Scherer, Vincent 56.2; Shakirov, Albert 42.1; Soelberg, Anna 56.3; Sriskandan, Kumar 50.1; Susie Bennett 17.1; Tack, Jochen 89.1; tommaso altamura 77.1; Van Lennep, Chris 56.4; Wheatley, Michael 23.1; Zoonar GmbH 93.1. |Alamy Stock Photo (RMB), Abingdon/Oxfordshire: Bachman, Bill 15.3; Ben Ari, Rafael 12.2; Bisgrove, Stephen 26.1; Borysovskyi, Iaroslav 19.1; Cuff, Tim 29.1; Cultura Creative RF 24.1; Gottschalk, Manfred 12.3; Long, Suzanne 12.1; Michael, Andrew 241.2; Mint Images Limited 60.1; Nicolas Menijes Crego 59.1; Paterson, Ian 20.1; Prostock-studio 49.1; robertharding 15.2; RTimages 33.1; Stamboulis, Dave 35.1; Vilata, Juan 29.2; Wall, David 15.1; Wiskerke, Wim 241.1. |Creative Listening, Newick: 43.1. |Donnelly, Karen, Brighton: 9.1, 28.1. |Getty Images, München: The AGE 11.1; Williams, Lisa Maree 11.2. |Imago, Berlin: Bluegreen Pictures 21.1. |iStockphoto.com, Calgary: AaronAmat 76.1; audioundwerbung 10.1; Constantinis 73.1; fcafotodigital 80.1; Fokusiert 71.1; pixdeluxe 30.1; pop_jop 7.1; Potemkin, Alex 69.1. |Shutterstock.com, New York: Andrjuss 72.1; Miceking 8.1; Pixel-Shot 37.1. |stock.adobe.com, Dublin: bramgino 6.1.

Audio credits

Dialogues and words and phrases produced by Anne Rosenfeld for RBA Productions (rbaproductions.co.uk). Recording engineer Mark Smith.

Video credits

Videos 1: produced by Anne Rosenfeld for RBA Productions, Brighton (rbaproductions.co.uk). Editor: David Rafique. Picture credits: simonbradfield / iStockphoto.com; Delbono, Maurizio / iStockphoto.com; Tierney, Darren / iStockphoto.com; omersukrugoksu / iStockphoto.com; PTW / iStockphoto.com; Gregs, David / Alamy Stock Photo; FaberrInk/ iStockphoto.com; Bridgeman Images; robertharding / Alamy Stock Photo; Tweedie, Penny / Alamy Stock Photo; MJ Photography / Alamy Stock Photo; FLHCAA1 / Alamy Stock Photo; 2d Alan King / Alamy Stock Photo; World History Archive / Alamy Stock Photo; public domain sourced / access rights from BNA Photographic / Alamy Stock Photo; The Print Collector / Alamy Stock Photo; De Agostini Picture Library / akg-images GmbH; Selwyn / Alamy Stock Photo; Lake Erie Maps and Prints / Alamy Stock Photo; benoitb / iStockphoto.com; IanDagnall Computing / Harris, Terry / Alamy Stock Photo; Colport / Alamy Stock Photo; public domain sourced / access rights from De Luan / Alamy Stock Photo; Steward, Linda / iStockphoto.com; Pictorial Press Ltd /

Alamy Stock Photo; Morrison, John / Alamy Stock Photo; public domain sourced / access rights from Lakeview Images / Alamy Stock Photo; Waters, Colin / Alamy Stock Photo; World History Archive / Alamy Stock Photo; Granger Historical Picture Archive / Alamy Stock Photo; public domain sourced / access rights from The Picture Art Collection / Alamy Stock Photo; zhencong chen / Alamy Stock Photo; Jones, David Keith / Alamy Stock Photo; public domain sourced / access rights from Atomic / Alamy Stock Photo; Daniren / Alamy Stock Photo

Video 2 + 3: produced by James Vyner and Luke Vyner for Creative Listening, London (www.creativelistening.co.uk)